COASTLINE OF CORNWALL

Ken Duxbury

BOSSINEY BOOKS

'. . . but don't in the least hurry the journey.
Better it last for years,
so that when you reach the island you are old,
rich with all you have gained on the way.'

Ithaca
(C.P. Cavafy)

First published in 1985
by Bossiney Books
St Teath, Bodmin, Cornwall.
Designed, printed and bound in Great Britain by
A. Wheaton & Co Ltd, Exeter, Devon

ISBN 0 948158 07 7

Plate Acknowledgements
Cover photography by Ken Duxbury
Peter Keeling: pages 24,39,43,46,74
Harry H. Ross LRPS: pages 4/5,7,31
Herbert Hughes (1903) by courtesy of Royal Institution of Cornwall: page 6
Photel Studios Ltd: pages 55,76
C. H. Vernon: page 19
Trevaunance Point Hotel: page 35
Tad Ciastula: page 36
Roy J. Westlake: page 64
Curnow Shipping Co: page 62
English China Clays Group: page 79
Plymouth City Museum and Art Gallery: page 60
HM Coastguard, Falmouth: page 75 left
All other photographs by the Author

Acknowledgements:
Production of a book is never just the work of the author: it involves many others who give their time, share their experiences and co-operate in innumerable ways. To all such I here convey my sincere thanks.

Specifically I would like to mention Peter Keeling who responded on more than one occasion to urgent calls for the use of his cameras, and Harry Ross LRPS who helped obviate many potential mistakes in my own photographic work as well as spending hours on windy Cornish cliffs giving valuable advice, then printing many of the monochrome enlargements. I would like also to thank Angela Thomas for so competently reading the proofs, and last but not least to thank Brenda my wife who designed the layout of the entire book while suffering me during the writing processes . . . only an author's wife can know what that means!

About the Author and the Book

Ken Duxbury has an unusually rich experience of seagoing which spans some 45 years. He joined the Royal Navy as an Ordinary Seaman in 1942, gained his commission shortly after, and attained command of one of HM ships before retiring from the Service in 1954 to found a highly successful sailing school on the north coast of Cornwall.

Author of ten books, he started writing in 1957 and has been a sailing contributor to the *Sunday Express* for 28 years. He married in 1963 and retired from business in 1970. In 1972 Brenda, his wife, crewed him in his small open sailing boat *Lugworm* for six months in Greece before helping him to sail the dinghy home to Cornwall.

Ken is now a full-time author and journalist, living at St Breward on Bodmin Moor. In 1984 he made his debut for Bossiney with *Sea Stories of Cornwall* hoisting the century for the Cornish cottage publishers. His love of Cornwall and unique experience of the coast is reflected in this his second Bossiney title, for, as he says in the Introduction: '. . . even on that first morning I believe I knew there was something quite extraordinary hidden in this sea-girt peninsula; something which resonated in harmony with my soul.'

The author and his boat Lugworm *on the set for the BBC TV series* Poldark.

Introduction

There was an explosion of light as the hatch slid back. Everywhere, far as eye could range, was colour, brilliance and space. A chuckle of waves lapped the hull of our boat, borne by a young west wind, and ashore broad swathes of green swept down to low cliffs whose rocky faces still glistened with the morning dew.

There were dark caves and long bouldered outcrops probing into deep water and just made for diving from . . . and close abeam the most perfect small sandy beach was tucked secretly under the brow of a shadowed cove which even now was in the process of awakening. I just sat and watched as a shaft of morning sunlight skidded over the clifftop to gently spread along the sand like a welcoming smile.

'Ted . . . Mu . . .' I bellowed down the hatch, 'come on deck, quick, for all unbeknown last night we dropped anchor in Paradise!'

That was over three decades ago when my errant sailor's spirit first took root in Cornwall, but even on that morning I believe I knew there was something quite extraordinary hidden in this sea-girt peninsula; something which resonated in harmony with my soul.

It had been an easy passage from South Wales. I remember the previous evening settling to my 'trick' at the helm while the horizon astern was still clearly distinguishable from the blue-black of a starry August sky. Lundy Isle light had winked its friendly 'goodbye' and the Gower coast was already a happy chapter slowly disappearing back there far beyond the end of our phosphorescent wake. Under the dark tan sails Hartland light provided the 'fix' to confirm that we were on track for Padstow, and *Thyra* my old Whitstable oysterboat sighed contentedly along with the light west wind which greeted the ebb tide

without unduly ruffling the sea's face. Ted, my friend and crew, together with his wife Mu, were 'off watch' and the delicious scent of sizzling bacon came from the teak hatch to where I lazed in the gathering dark, my hand on the long curved tiller.

Cornwall ahead. An unknown coast, for none of we three had yet explored farther than north Somerset in the old forty-foot cutter. Now we were extending our horizons . . . maybe even to 'round The Land' if the weather held fair. There was no urgency: our voyaging was always 'for the riches gained on the way' and never for frenzy of competition or out of desperation to gain some destination.

With the ebb tide helping us westward we were due to arrive off Pentire Point at the mouth of the Camel estuary well before dawn, and low water at that, which boded ill for crossing the infamous Doom Bar. So we huddled over the chart and agreed to drop anchor in Portquin Bay snug under the lee of Rumps Point and The Mouls islet while waiting for the Bristol Channel to fill up again. The moon gave light for us to skirt close along the shore with confidence, and we only lost the wind as we rounded-up to let go anchor in five fathoms right beside Compit. While the boat settled to her chain our eyes scanned this dark new land – no more than a vague silhouette against the night sky. Trevose was hidden by the bulk of Pentire and there was no glimmer of light anywhere to be seen. The forecast was set fair, so all three of us turned in, tired but contentedly alert, for you sleep with your ears wide awake when afloat.

It is always exciting to come on deck after a good night's sleep and see an anchorage or harbour for the first time by the light of a new day. But none of us quite expected this! We had voyaged down with the ebb and now, looking at this coast it seemed almost as though time itself had known an ebb and withdrawn back into an earlier age when Earth was younger. An almost archetypal freshness charged the scene. Unconsciously, even then, I knew this was to become my home. From Marsland Mouth where the Cornish border gently nudges Devon out of the way, along those magnificent cliffs under Morwenstow to the wide sweep of Bude Bay and the breathtaking grandeur of the old quarry workings at Trebarwith and Tintagel . . . these were to be my introduction to more extended explorations far along the whole north and south coasts right to the 'end of The Land'. Ever since, on foot, afloat, and in the air, this coast and its people have fascinated me.

Of course a book of this nature, written by one author alone, must bear the stamp of that author's perceptions and interests. It may be the present book is coloured by a sailor's eye. So be it: I am grateful to Michael Williams for making it possible for me to include here many of my personal impressions. Just as one may read the lines etched by time on a much-loved face so, on the shores of Cornwall I have learned to read and interpret that ceaseless dialogue of sea with land. It is a dialogue that has been continuous since Earth was created, and in the process has fashioned this coastline into a magnificent stage fit to play host to the elemental moods of nature. In like manner too, I believe it has fashioned the Cornish people.

For many readers I hope this book will be a voyage of discovery and adventure. For the countless thousands who flock to these shores each summer for one magicial week or fortnight it may bring nostalgic memories – for they, too, have caught the echo of Cornwall's song, and once that subtle melody has stirred the soul there is no forgetting.

To such, here in pictures, this coastline will speak for itself. If, in the accompanying words, there is shared one tiny part of the happiness, adventure and awe it has brought the writer, the book will be more than worthwhile. Should the total experience be encapsulated in a single word, that word would be FREEDOM.

Low tide St Ives (left). Boats may change but the harbours retain their atmosphere. Padstow harbour today (right).

Pearl Dyer
SUSY O
91

I
Marsland Mouth to Padstow

From Hartland point to Padstow bay
is a sailor's grave by night or day.

To begin then at the beginning. There is a little stream very full of its own importance chattering along in a small wooded valley which cuts steeply down this northern coast to emerge at Marsland Mouth. This stream, which is called Marsland Water, starts life some two or three miles inland, a mere half of one of Tregeagle's demented leaps from the source of the noble Tamar up near Crim and Eastcott.

Marsland Water is just a ditch up there on the watershed, but gains in stature as it wriggles westward down past Gooseham Mill and from thence, in winter, one may with truth call it a brook for it chuckles to itself as though it were keeping a secret. It is: there is Devon water and Cornish water all bubbling together and flowing ever more urgently between steep coppice-studded banks until, with a final exultant rush, it bounces and froths over the grey slate boulders at the Mouth. There, with all-too-evident shock, it is knocked back again halfway up the shingle by the hissing Atlantic breakers.

Be it this urgent torrent in mid winter or just a lazy trickle in hot summer, nevertheless Marsland Water is unique for it does mark the boundary between Devon and Cornwall – a fact which, some fifty yards or so from the beach is proclaimed to the affronted gulls by a truly hideous metal reflective roadsign

'No more glorious place than this bracing northern shore . . .' Left: Sailing out of the Camel estuary. Right: Rumps Point from Pentire Head.

'Marsland Water . . . bounces and froths over the grey slate boulders at the Mouth.'

KERNOW-CORNWALL which looks as much at home in this otherwise unspoilt valley as would a plastic garden gnome at Sothebys. I heartily wish some gallant Cornishman would uproot the thing and cast it far into the Atlantic, replacing it by a solid inscribed slab of honest Delabole slate! But I digress.

Sign or not, make no mistake as you cross this stream on the coastal footpath you are setting foot on the very bulwarks of this our sceptred isle, for there is nothing else keeping the great ocean at bay save our rocky peninsula. What better way to digest that fact than to turn southward and immediately climb the steep valley side to Marsland Cliff. From here your eye may glide as a bird flies along Cornakey and Henna cliffs, over more steep valleys and onward some ten miles, ranging as it does along a coast the like of which will shiver the timbers of your soul, so rugged and elemental is it. Ironbound, sailors have called it, and it does seem to have exerted a sort of death-wish to mariners across the centuries, for many a fine ship trying to round Hartland just to the northward has ended her life and that of her crew on these unforgiving rocks. Black, grey and shot with russet mineral, ironbound it truly is, hanging over breakers in four-hundred foot high cliffs which throw up a constant mist of tears from broken-hearted swells.

But only in winter.

In summer, why, there is no more glorious place to keep fit and young than this bracing northern shore. You may cool off, taking the breath from a thousand miles of ocean on each clifftop, then run down into any of these secret valleys out of the wind, and lie sunbathing there, untroubled, secluded and free in the warmth, soaking in the pineapple scent of gorse and musky heather, watching the predatory sweep of a buzzard maybe, or the focused concentration of a sparrowhawk. Seaward, where the tiny freshwater streams leap in their final drop to the beach, fulmars, kittiwakes and greybacks soar and chatter to join with you in the sheer joy of being alive.

Such is the magic of this coastline. One lives more intensely here, and all who come to these shores without discovering it are surely dead already in their souls. Others have known it across history and some of them have expressed the fact with words or in their lives with an eloquence that has echoed through time.

One such was the charismatic Robert Stephen Hawker, vicar of Morwenstow from 1834 until just before his death in 1875. This larger-than-life character rebuilt the vicarage which nestles close under the church of Morwenstow three valleys away. The house is worth viewing for its eccentric chimneys alone, modelled on the churches with which he had been associated – all, that is, except the kitchen chimney which is a replica of his mother's tomb.

A kind and compassionate man, yet Hawker never dodged the harsh realities of life and knew tragedy at close quarters. Much of his time was spent recovering the dreadfully dismembered bodies of drowned seamen, victims of local shipwreck. Go to the churchyard today, calling if it pleases you at the excellent and haunted Bush Inn, and you will see just up the bank inside the church gate a fitting memorial to one such, the *Caledonia* of Arbroath. She was a two-hundred ton vessel that drove ashore in a storm of 1842 and the 'gravestone' is her actual figurehead, a carved-wood Caledonian warrior complete with sword and shield, albeit somewhat bereft of physiognomy, but so would you be had you weathered those rocks and the Cornish gales for a century or more. There he stands, still guarding the grave of all but one of the vessel's crew. Hawker himself buried them, including the captain, and brought the figurehead from the beach to place it there. Mind you the figure has a fascinating history and a very odd reputation. But it speaks volumes for the compassion of the local folk that it has, more-or-less, remained there for well over 140 years. To gain an insight into the soul of this remarkable vicar you should get from the library a copy of Joan Rendell's book *Hawker Country* also published by Bossiney, which is now, alas, out of

'This coast does seem to have exerted a sort of death-wish to mariners.' Two lost their lives in this wreck.

Hawker's hut on Vicarage cliff. The view undoubtedly inspired him to write so movingly of this ironbound coast (right).

print, or the booklet *Robert Stephen Hawker of Morwenstow, a Belated Mediaeval* by A. L. Rowse, published by Elephant Press.

Hawker liked nothing better than to walk across the field from his church to these clifftops – a mere quarter of a mile or so – and there to sit reflecting and gazing down the awesome drop to those rockstrewn beaches below. So attached did he become to the view that he built himself a small wooden hide-away under the brow of what is now called Vicarage Cliff, and you may be sure it was here, while listening to the ceaseless roar below that he drafted his short poem *The Figurehead of the Caledonia at her Captain's Grave*:

We laid them in their lowly rest,
The strangers of a distant shore;
We smoothed the green turf on their breast
Mid baffled ocean's angry roar:
and there, the relique of the storm
We fixed fair Scotland's figured form.

Tennyson himself visited Hawker in 1848, for this remarkable vicar was becoming a legend in his own time. You may sit in his hide-away today, refraining I do beseech you from adding to the irrelevant names carved on the timberwork, and share the magnificent view that undoubtedly influenced his thinking, profound and worthy soul that he must have been to

From Morwenstow the coast plummets five miles due south to Bude.

write such thoughts as: 'Paradise! How lovely must its fields have been since Earth, the land of our exile, is so surpassingly fair.' The insight reminds me strongly of that brilliant parable of *The Islanders* at the introduction to Idries Shah's book *The Sufis*. Hawker knew a thing or two.

From Morwenstow the coast plummets five miles straight as a meridian due south to Bude, though you might wear out a pair of stout bootsoles traversing it and become intimate with the composition of the land. The main body of Cornwall is exposed in the granite knobbles of her spine, notably at Hingston Down, Kit Hill, Bodmin Moor, St Austell, Penryn and Land's End. But excepting between St Ives and Land's End this granite rarely shows itself at the coast which is largely slate. In fact the granite breaks through rather like islands in a sea of slate. From the Devon border down to Boscastle however, the coast is mostly dark coloured shales which the Cornish call 'killas'. The chief difference is that shale tends to split along lines which follow the plane of its original deposition, while real slate will split more along lines coincident with the pressure which caused its impaction.

If you want to study the geological structure and actually see the stratified layers of rock which were once deep under the sea but, since Paleozoic times have been heaved up, marvellously curved and crumpled by Earth's changing facial expression, you cannot do better than walk this piece of the coast, for it is laid out here in the cliffs like a book to be read in layers, each a page spanning millenia.

But the wonderful stretches of sand which are revealed at low water from Menachurch Point near Northcott down to Bude Haven itself are much softer on the eye and foot. At low water equinoctial spring tides you will be fit and thirsty if you jog all the way down at the ocean's edge to Wrangle Point and Crooklets Beach under Flexbury. Take heed though; study the rise and fall of the tide everywhere on this coast, for it is all too easy for those who are uninitiated to get caught as the sea-level rises fifteen feet or more. It happens all too often, and we end up risking our own lives, not to mention those of the rescue services as they draw a frightened casualty up some unscaleable cliff-face!

You will, as I say, be quite ready for a cup of good cheer at one of the fine hotels or pubs in Bude, which has a pleasant spacious ambience all of its own. There is an air of lingering gentility about this north coast resort with its castle on the small promontory backing the fine golden beach. The meandering River Neet greets the sea hand-in-hand as it were with the famous Bude Canal whose final lock-gate forms a bastion against the Bristol Channel, holding the canal water back to provide a small picturesque harbour.

There is much to do in Bude, for the town has an innovative and forward-looking Council which has been instrumental in using the Manpower Services Commission in the construction of a 'Trim Trail' across local meadows. This is to create opportunities and enthusiasm for 'jogging' combined with an informal series of prescribed exercises undertaken at selected spots in very attractive settings. At each 'station' the exercises are carefully worked out to cater for specific muscles of which you may well become aware for the first time, and you follow a colour code to progress gently and, it is hoped enjoyably, to higher standards of fitness. So Bude holidaymakers return home not only thoroughly relaxed and happy, but much fitter to boot! The town has a splendid museum which includes models and photographs of shipwrecks hereabouts, and you may also learn much of the natural history of the area and its geology.

North Door on Strangles beach which leads through to the remarkable quartz and slate chequerboard (below right).

So we follow the coastal footpath southward toward Widemouth Bay, thence past Millook Haven and on to the magnificent headland at Crackington Haven from where, if you still have any breath left, you may climb still more west and southward round Cambeak Point and beyond. Shortly, if you aren't day-dreaming in the summer haze, you will find a narrow cliff path deflecting seaward beneath awe-inspiring buttresses which look as though they are about to avalanche into the sea – and they probably are – so don't linger here, but run on down some four or more hundred feet to the incomparable shingly beach known as The Strangles. How it got the name I cannot imagine, for there could be no more inappropriate spot to strangle anyone, nor yet to be strangled. Only at half-tide and below is there any sand exposed, and then only at the middle and southern end.

The north end of this mile-and-a-half long beach is separated by a remarkable natural arch of convoluted rock known as North Door. As you pass through it, nine times out of ten there will be a raucation of screaming gulls, strident and echoing above you and not infrequently unloading a cargo of 'good luck' just to warn that care must be taken, for if the tide rises you will not pass back through that arch, and may have to wait many hours for the sea-level to fall again. But once through it there is a wonderful display of quartz chequerboard on a great horizontal slab of slate. I firmly believe it is where Neptune plays noughts and crosses when it is covered by the tide, and if I tell you I have seen sea-nymphs as nature made them playing hop-scotch there, would you believe me?

Can you think of any better way to spend a summer day than sunbathing and swimming, or maybe just wallowing in the weedy rock pools while hunting crabs, then reclimbing that wonderful cliff path where suddenly, after the ceaseless roar of the breakers there is a profound and almost tangible silence in a remarkable sound-shadow. So you may wander the quarter of a mile or so to Trevigue Farm

Trevigue farm where, on a cloistered lawn you may indulge in as fine a Cornish cream tea as you will get anywhere in the area.

where, on a suntrapping, cloistered, grassy lawn, you may indulge in as fine a Cornish cream tea as you will get anywhere in the area. Afterwards, if you are lucky and they are not already fully booked, you may stay the night there in the beautifully modernised rooms which still retain the atmosphere of olden times, and have a hearty breakfast before setting off southward again.

Make no mistake, there is romance and atmosphere by the basketful in Cornwall. Legends and myths abound, some based on fact, many pure imagination. But all have one quality in common: they fulfil a deep-rooted need in the human psyche. One such, and surely supreme, is the legend of Arthur and his Knights, sited here at Tintagel by Geoffrey of Monmouth, and told by Sir Thomas Malory, Tennyson and others down the centuries. They chose as a stage for the events the cliffbound headland here close by the ancient Church of St Materiana. Have you walked across the bridge which now spans that chasm to the island? Have you passed through those crumbling ruins of the once great Norman castle and gazed out to sea, wondering at the meaning hidden in those stories? Have you gone down to sea-level and stood inside Merlin's Cave

'Have you passed through those crumbling ruins of the once great Norman castle?'

there beneath the castle, and dwelt on the profound symbolism of the young King-to-be who, alone of all the contenders, was able to 'withdraw the sword from the stone'? The stories are a remarkable flight of human understanding and insight, indicating as they do the direction for future development of humankind. You will not do better than to take a book of the legends with you, and sit at evening reliving the epics on the top of Glebe Cliff beneath the church wall.

Summer and romance, sunbathing, swimming and all the lotus-eating that goes with carefree holidaymaking is for many the very essence of Cornwall. But it is far from being the whole story. Indeed, on that magical morning when we first anchored in Portquin Bay and marvelled at the beauty of the scene, little did I think that a quarter of a century later I would stand huddled with a small and apprehensive group, leaning against the fury of a westerly storm and watching the final hours of a small coaster which had fallen foul of the ironbound coast when in unforgiving mood.

It was at 9.30 a.m. on 15 December 1979 that Hartland Coastguard picked up a relayed 'Mayday' signal by radio from a British ship reporting that another vessel some three miles north of Trevose Head was not under command due to heavy weather. 'Mayday' is the English equivalent of the French words *M'Aidez* — Help me! — and is internationally recognised as a signal of distress at sea. 'Not under command' is the phrase used at sea for any ship which is manoeuvring with difficulty.

Four minutes later Land's End radio repeated the distress call and identified the disabled ship as the Greek coaster *Skopelos Sky* bound from Rotterdam to Liverpool. Immediately the Padstow lifeboat was launched from the slipway at the north end of Mother Ivey's Bay just east of Trevose Head, and a helicopter at the Royal Naval Air Station, Culdrose, alerted.

The weather conditions off this north coast that day were frightful. A force ten northwesterly wind was knocking up mountainous breaking seas, and when the captain of *Skopelos Sky* reported that he was operating with reduced power on his engine it was clear to all that a major tragedy was quite possible. He further reported that he had fifteen lives aboard, and at the time was capable of making at most a laboured seven knots. It had been his intention to seek shelter on the northern shore of the Bristol Channel, but conditions had forced him ever more southerly along this north coast and it was his desperate hope to find some shelter where he could anchor and ride out the storm. At 9.42 a.m. he reported his ship as having a dangerous list due to shifting cargo, and requested helicopter assistance to take off some crew.

It is from this moment that the true value of a network of instant communication and close teamwork between the different rescue services becomes clear. Hartland Coastguard took over co-ordination from Land's End radio, who reported that helicopters were already being sent from RAF Chivenor and Brawdy. RNAS Culdrose was temporarily affected by storm damage and unable to respond immediately.

Rocky Valley near Tintagel.

By ten o'clock Padstow lifeboat was sighting the coaster intermittently between grey mountains of blown spume, about quarter of a mile away. A Whirlwind rescue helicopter number 69 was speeding from Chivenor, another Sea-king helicopter number 90 was racing toward the scene from Brawdy, and a third helicopter Wessex 21 was airborne from Culdrose. In addition the Port Isaac Coastguard had the vessel in sight and had the full coastal rescue team together with all their equipment speeding in their Land Rover to Portquin Bay.

Hartland was now communicating with the stricken

By first light of dawn Skopelos Sky *had broken in half.*

coaster via Padstow lifeboat which was keeping the ship close company, though quite unable in the ferocious conditions to go alongside.

At 10.30 a.m., Whirlwind 69, Sea-King 90 and Wessex 21 were hovering above *Skopelos Sky* whose master requested that immediate 'lift-off' of some crew members might commence. Sea-King 90, looking like a fat dragonfly hovering incredibly near to the wallowing ship, in a series of remarkable 'lifts' took off ten of the crew, landing them at St Mawgan without any injuries. Five crew remained aboard, which doubtless eased the mind of her Master who knew that it was a very tricky situation indeed but reported that he still had some power and was not calling for the assistance of a tug. By this time the ship was as close as seamanship allowed to the shore under Rumps Point. There was no possibility of entering Padstow in the exceptional sea conditions. His only hope was to drop anchor and then ease the enormous strain on the cable by holding her head-to-wind and sea with the engine. Whirlwind 69 returned to Chivenor. Hartland and the military at Plymouth held a discussion and agreed that Sea-King 90 should also return to Brawdy and revert to one hour's notice. Wessex 21 was instructed to remain on the clifftop at Portquin at immediate alert so as to save fuel.

By now it was past midday and the Port Isaac Coastguard reported the weather on the scene as north-north-westerly wind force ten gusting to force twelve, with rain showers. That is a full storm, gusting to hurricane force, and even for this coast a rarity. At 1.50 p.m. lifeboat 70-003 at Lundy Island was instructed to relieve the Padstow lifeboat which looked like a cork being flung about in that murderous waste of grey-green Hell.

Meanwhile, aboard, it was the stated intention of the Master to save his vessel if at all possible without further assistance. But the problem of failing light was looming. A three-way discussion took place between Plymouth, Hartland and Culdrose on the practicability if needed, for a helicopter rescue after dark. It was decided that in the existing conditions this would be unacceptably hazardous. The Master, the owners, and the ship's agents were advised of the situation.

Just before 4 p.m., with the light fading fast, the Master reported that he intended dropping anchor in Portquin Bay and that, whether he was successful or not in getting an effective anchor down, he would like the remaining four crew lifted off while some light remained. You must understand that in those conditions to even send a man forward along the deck of the vessel to the anchor-winch was itself highly dangerous. The ship was 'submarining' at times under the onslaught of enormous waves . . . but it was achieved at 4.13 p.m.

At 4.20 p.m. the Wessex 21, having topped-up with fuel again at St Mawgan, was overhead and preparing to winch off more men. It was an anxious time, with many eyes watching to see whether the anchor could possibly hold in the maelstrom, and the Master alone on board. Sea-King 90 had once more returned to the scene, and to all concerned it was quite clear that the anchor was not holding . . . *Skopelos Sky*, with every heave of the ocean, was coming relentlessly toward the shore. As she did so the lifeboat had to stand off, for the breaking seas within quarter of a mile of the cliffs were a sight to behold.

At 5.15 p.m., in the very last of the light, she drove onto the rocks, and even as she did so Sea-King 90

Few summer visitors guess the fury of our winter seas. Portquin, March 1984.

winched the Master up, and flew him safely to St Mawgan. Both Padstow and Lundy lifeboats returned to their stations, and by the first light of dawn *Skopelos Sky* had broken in half, her stern section a pathetic sight lying helplessly battered by the swells, and her foreparts firmly jammed under the cliff of Doyden Point. She broke up very quickly, releasing her cargo of lub-oil drums, paint and other materials, but thank heaven the ninety or so tons of diesel fuel in her tanks did not cause any appreciable pollution of the coast.

The realities of life are dramatic enough, but the Cornish coastline has the power of stimulating the imagination of writers and film-makers alike, lending itself to realistic backdrops so little has it changed across the ages. *Jamaica Inn*, *Rebecca*, and the famous *Poldark* novels were sited here and Winston Graham in the latter works was inspired by the names of Cornish villages to lend realism to his characters. Television producers shot some of the scenes for the epic *Poldark* series in the tiny haven of Portquin and the local populace – including myself – had days of fun and interest dressing up as 'extras' in period costume, walking the carefully disguised 'dirt track' – in fact the metalled roadway spread thick with straw and earth – in front of the old fish cellars. Foliage was brought to disguise telegraph poles as trees, modern litter baskets hastily buried under lobster-pots, and where telephone lines intruded despite all efforts – why, simply take a handful of clothes-pegs and make them into laundry-lines!

The sheer ingenuity and good-humour of those film-makers was a lesson in itself. Even the redoubtable *Lugworm*, the writer's sailing dinghy, was brought into service landing the 'fish' catch while the locals, including yours truly, were bewitched by the full-blooded vamping of 'Emma' played by Trudy Styler. Winston Graham himself joined in, watching it all from a lobster-pot seat alongside the slipway, and what great-hearted fun it all was!

A far cry from real storm and shipwreck, but before we leave the less enchanting aspects of life on the coast, do you know that every year some 7,000 people are helped in one way or another by the Coastguard and Lifeboat services around the coast of the UK? Of these, only a tiny three per cent involve

Poldark *at Portquin: the good humour of the film-makers (above) was a lesson in itself. Local boats (below) were brought into service, while (opposite) Trudy Styler captured all male hearts while playing 'Emma'.*

merchant shipping while twenty-five per cent result from small pleasure craft getting into difficulty, and a staggering thirty-one per cent involves shore search and rescue. It is, in fact, the ignorance and thoughtlessness of holidaymakers which gives the rescue authorities their biggest headache. To meet this latter need the RNLI have developed a very effective organisation of small, fast, inflatable inshore lifeboats driven by powerful outboard motors, and it is these, crewed by local volunteers, which speed to the source of trouble when minutes can literally mean life or death.

A good example of this took place close south of Tintagel Head on 26 August 1983. It was 7.21 p.m. when David Castle, secretary of the Port Isaac inshore lifeboat, got a report from the Coastguard that two people were cut off by the rising tide at Hole Beach, Trebarwith, some five miles up the coast. Although the weather was fair and one might have expected the rescue personnel to be 'off their guard' so to speak, in fact there was no need to fire the maroons because, as is their habit, both secretary and crew were all casually listening-in to communications between the Maritime Rescue Co-ordination Centre at Falmouth and the Boscastle Coastal Rescue Team. These men are never really off-duty, and always on the alert.

Inside Port Isaac harbour there was little swell and no sea running, the wind being a mere seven knots or so from a northerly direction. Visibility was good, and within five minutes of hearing the distress report the sixteen-foot 'D' class inflatable with its forty horsepower outboard was launched and speeding from harbour. Barry Slater (41) the helmsman, accompanied by Harry Pavitt (39) and John Trayhurn (33) expected little trouble in getting to the two trapped holidaymakers. High tide that evening was at eight o'clock, so there was only half an hour before high water. In that time the tide would not rise appreciably.

As they left the harbour the speaker of their powerful VHF radio crackled into life: about one quarter of a mile beyond Hole Beach at Penhallick Point a woman had just been washed off the rocks. There was an unmistakable sense of urgency now in David Castle's voice as more detailed reports came in. Another holidaymaker, seeing the woman's plight, had courageously plunged in to give assistance. Out there in the open sea as the inflatable surf-rode the waves it was quite clear that there was a much bigger swell running into those beaches than had been thought. All along Tregardock and Trebarwith they could see the white mist of lifting spray where the swells broke with thunderous roar. Anyone attempting to scramble ashore on those rocks – which the rescue crew knew well – stood little chance of survival. This emergency was of a different calibre to the original call; seconds might well count.

The Port Isaac inshore lifeboat was launched within five minutes of receiving the distress call.

When the skipper opens up the engine to give full power on these inflatable lifeboats, it is no longer a question of being afloat: the entire boat is a skimming surfboard that literally leaps across the waves. To remain unharmed one has to adopt a particular posture while kneeling so as to lessen the shock of the hammer-blows as the boat slaps down, then leaps again to 'fly' – sometimes literally free of the surface – to the next wave. It is a skill that only comes with practice, and meanwhile the crew must be on full alert to hear any new instructions coming over the radio from base, and also to navigate the craft unerringly to the casualty area.

As they sped towards Penhallick Point the swells built up in height due to the shallowing seabed. Barry Slater casting an eye astern, assessed the rank upon rank of swell-crests advancing inexorably towards the shore. Seamen learn to read the ocean. There are periods when these swells diminish in size, and then periods of about equal length when they grow again. It is imperative that one choose exactly the right moment to go in close to recover casualties. Barry eased the power off as they neared the area, and then they simultaneously sighted two dark objects very close to the rocks. It turned out to be the head of the man who had jumped in to assist, and a spherical lobster-pot buoy onto which he was holding with one hand. Though they could not at that moment see it, he had his other arm round the woman. As each successive swell reached them, building up to break with enormous force on the rocks beyond, the heads disappeared under water.

'I reckon,' said John Trayhurn, 'another couple of minutes and they would have been "goners". We scooped them both aboard and found the woman badly lacerated from her attempts to regain the shore. They were both suffering from exposure and shock, so we wrapped them in blankets to retain their warmth.'

Meanwhile, ashore, the back-up team had not been idle. A rescue helicopter was speeding to the area from Chivenor, piloted by Flight Lieutenant Mike Douglas. No sooner had first-aid been applied than this was hovering overhead, with Larry Evans the winchman dropping down on the end of the thin wire to connect with the stationary lifeboat. At 7.55 p.m. both rescued persons were being whisked to Stratton hospital. Which still left the two original trapped people on Hole Beach wondering what was going on!

'We could see them huddled on the rocks in the mouth of the huge shallow cave which gives the beach its name,' Barry explained. 'I reckon they had walked round the rocky point from Trebarwith beach without realising the tide was rising, and too late discovered they were cut off. Long before the tide would have receded again it would have been dark and very dangerous to attempt a return round that point.'

After careful appraisal he took the lifeboat straight in 'on the back of a swell' to ground on a flat rock which every now and then dried out as the swell receded. This is an extremely difficult and tricky manoeuvre calling for split-second timing, but these men are experienced by constant training in just such action. As the boat dropped down on the rock John and Harry leapt out, got their footing and swung the boat's bow right round to face seaward, so as to take the next breaker 'on the nose'. As she floated again they allowed her, under control, to be swept back to yet shallower rocks where she could be safely left for a brief moment while they attended to the casualties. They once more turned out to be a man and woman, the latter suffering from abrasions. After giving first aid they got the woman aboard – the man elected to remain ashore until the tide fell and a shore rescue team could reach him.

Now started the immensely more tricky business of getting afloat again and clear of the rocks. One cannot physically lift a seventeen-hundredweight boat and carry it with an injured person aboard across massive boulders which are intermittently covered by breakers; the sea itself has to do the lifting and this is why the timing is so critical. But it's one thing to drive a boat ashore, choosing exactly the right moment to run in with the waves behind you. It is quite another to re-float on the surge of a wave, get the outboard propeller lowered, start the engine and get free of the rocks into deep water without any damage. They had very nearly made it, with Harry and John up to their

Barry Slater (left), Harry Pavitt and, (front) John Trayhurn, crew of the Port Isaac inshore lifeboat on 26 August 1983.

waists in the breakers and Barry all set to turn on power, when disaster struck. The propeller hit the rocks just as the other two pulled themselves back aboard. The inflatable swung across the next advancing wave, and boat, crew and casualty were lifted high to be swept back far up the foreshore, where they were left more-or-less high and dry as that one rogue wave receded.

Try as they might, it was impossible to manhandle the boat back to the point from which a second re-launch could be attempted. To do so would, in addition, probably unnecessarily endanger the casualty. 'It was now,' interposed David Castle, who is also Watchman in Charge of the Port Isaac Coastguard Unit, 'that I received the classic signal from the cave mouth . . . terse . . . undramatic . . . but conveying precisely what we needed to know:
'Harry Pavitt to Port Isaac Coastguard.

Portquin bay with the Mouls isle. I little thought when I first anchored here and marvelled at the tranquil beauty of the scene that, some three decades later I would stand on this shore huddled against the fury of a storm while watching the last moments of a ship on the rocks below.

The casualties are all safe.
We have slight problem and cannot unaided get the lifeboat out of Hole Beach.
We await the return of the helicopter.'

David smiled at the recollection. 'We now had two separate problems,' he explained. 'First and most important, we had to somehow get the woman out of it and to hospital. Secondly, we had to get more manpower to bring the lifeboat safely off. The helicopter was due to return, and would deal with the first problem. I contacted the launching authority for the offshore lifeboat, requesting that she be launched from her slipway at Trevose Head. This was advisable in the circumstances, since she could then stand by to give any assistance that might be needed. I then organised a party of six volunteers from Port Isaac to go down on to the beach adjacent by a difficult cliff path, await the falling of the tide, and round the point to help lift the inflatable lifeboat into the water.'

'Meanwhile,' Barry continued, 'the helicopter was throbbing towards us out of sight above the cliff. We saw her come into sight and hover there . . . almost it seemed she was landing on the cliff edge, and we began to realise what a difficult task the pilot faced. To get a winchman down near enough to us, grouped as we were actually in the cave mouth with the waves breaking round about, he would have to bring the 'chopper' right into the cliff face. It was awe-inspiring to watch. That machine kept coming down . . . down . . . right into the cliff so it seemed. I believe there was not more than two or three feet between the ends of her rotor blades and the cliff face when it just hovered there like a huge sparrowhawk, and down came the winchman, swinging gently like a pendulum towards and away from the cliff until he dangled just above the breakers. We waded out, grabbed him and pulled him towards the woman, slipped the harness round her and they were away . . . up and over the clifftop and we were left in sudden silence.

'But we had our own problem still. We had to get

Ferry Point, Rock.

Trevor England, coxswain of Padstow Lifeboat.

SUSY D

Padstow Mayday. Great fun as we greet the return of spring!

the inflatable lifeboat and the uninjured man out of the situation, and darkness was on us. We knew that with the falling tide we could guide the man round the point with torches and back up the steep cliff path. But the falling tide left the boat ever farther from the water. We were glad to see the volunteer team of muscle-power, but I can tell you it wasn't easy in the darkness with those breakers. The offshore lifeboat was by now on the scene, and close inshore, coxswained by Trevor England. They shot a rocket-line across to us and we pulled over a stout rope. Helped by the shoreside team we manhandled her to the water, leapt aboard and gave the signal for Trevor to steam full-power seaward . . . we were off in moments!'

'Sounds easy?' laughed John, 'but I can tell you more than a few of us were up to our necks in foam before she was out of danger. Our propeller was slightly bent, so we all piled into the offshore boat and towed the inshore boat into Port Isaac. We all went off "alert" at half-past midnight.'

'Not a bad night's work really,' chuckled David. 'Four people rescued, and only very minor damage to the inshore boat, with no harm to any of the rescue personnel. I've known worse!' What David didn't know — nor at that time any of those involved — was that as a result of identifying an unknown yacht in Portquin Bay while on passage to Hole Beach, Trevor England in the offshore lifeboat was instrumental in preventing over half a million pounds worth of cocaine reaching its potential distributors, and two men went to jail.

But that is another story, and if you want to read the incredible but true sequence of events which befell out there due to that chance meeting at sea, you must buy my book *Sea Stories of Cornwall* published by Bossiney Books. You would hardly believe what goes on round here!

Padstow is well known by a multitude of holidaymakers, perhaps most especially for its famous 'Obby 'Oss which is 'teased' around the streets on the first day of May each year. It is a remarkable event,

Great changes have taken place in the small village of Rock. Sid Rodda watches demolition of the old Rock Hotel.

and one which is entered into with relish and gusto by all concerned. The streets are garlanded with green branches, and a huge maypole erected round which the children and others dance to the hypnotic beat of that strangely gripping rhythm. Meanwhile the weird black 'Oss gyrates, lunges, bows and follows the wildly dancing 'teaser' along the streets. It is the nearest thing I have seen in Europe to the Voodoo dances of African Witchdoctors, and goes

St Enodoc Church and the new grave of the Poet Laureate Sir John Betjeman . . . a peaceful setting on the coast he so dearly loved.

back in time across forgotten centuries. Somewhere, in the mists of time gone, it is connected with fertility rites, and certainly there is a remarkable energy and dynamic power abroad in those streets as we greet the return of spring, and the upsurge of growth and renewal of life.

This little port is unique in that it lies well up a shallow, sandy estuary, and it is this, in my opinion, which gives the place its character. Excessive commercial activity is virtually barred by the fact that this estuary has a shallow sandbank running right across its mouth. The famous Doom Bar precludes any vessels of deep draught coming into the port, so it is frequented mostly by fishing boats and pleasure yachts. This, together with the really beautiful stretches of golden sand which flank both sides of the estuary, make it a very popular holiday resort.

Over the last decade or so the moorings for small pleasure craft have been greatly extended on the Rock side of the estuary opposite Padstow. This has, of course, brought considerable change to the small village of Rock. But two things remain virtually the same: the famous 'Rock Wall' overlooking the estuary and the Sailing Clubhouse on the picturesque quay. That wall could tell many a tale, for it was, and still is, the haunt of the locals out of season, and the collecting-place for all and everyone during the season. The old Rock Hotel, focal point of the area for many generations, was demolished in the mid seventies, but the 'wall' remains, and so does the character of the place, which is famous for its dinghy sailing. Indeed it would be hard to imagine a more beautiful seascape than the view from the top of Cassock Hill just near the pedestrian ferry-landing.

The whole of the east side of the estuary is preserved by the well-known St Enodoc Golf Club, and tucked away in the green dunes is the little church of St Enodoc where lies the grave of that much-loved Poet Laureate Sir John Betjeman. It was Trebetherick, Daymer Bay, and the incomparable dunes of Brea beach that he most liked to roam, and it forms a beautiful, peaceful, and absolutely right setting for his last resting place, so near to his home.

II
Padstow to Godrevy Light

There is a wondrous blowhole (above) in Tregudda Gorge (opposite).

This area is dear to my own heart, for it is from the Camel estuary that I have explored the northern coast in my dinghy *Lugworm*. Just round Stepper Point, about half a mile down the coast there is a magnificent cleft in the rocks where a whole chunk of the land cracked off then changed its mind and stayed half at sea, leaving a gorge known locally as Tregudda. From it you may see the old cylindrical stone daymark looking much like the chimney of a disused mine, but in fact erected simply to mark the entrance to Padstow harbour.

Stories abound hereabouts of wreckers in olden times luring ships ashore by placing false lights on the clifftops. Baring-Gould, in his classic book *The Roar of the Sea* plays upon the theme which commences with the parson being lowered into St Enodoc Church through the roof, for it is a fact that the tiny building was once all but buried in the shifting sands. These wrecker tales may have some basis of truth in them, but my own experience of the Cornish people is quite the reverse; far more ready to jeopardise their own lives in attempting to save others, than otherwise. However, this bit of coast does have a reputation for wrecking in olden times, though I'm convinced it was just a matter of an 'eye for a profit' after the vessel had run ashore.

There is a wondrous blowhole in Tregudda gorge. A subterranean cave runs beneath the chunk of the cliffs which cracked off, and at the right state of tide when a good swell is rolling in, it builds up enormous pressure inside the cave and expels air and spray with a roar like a foghorn. It is as though some gigantic whale were blowing, and great fun to sit on

Scoured by the equinoctial tides and swept by winter winds, Harlyn Bay, host to a conference of gulls, prepares for the coming season (left) while Trevose lighthouse (above) stands guard close-by.

the rocks down to leeward and cool off in the salt shower . . . though somewhat tricky landing safely and not to be recommended unless you have the knack. At dead low water spring equinoctial tide I have swum through this cave and emerged in the gorge itself, but my guess is that it would be safe to do this about once every hundred years, for you have to catch it just right with the sea like a mirror.

Between Trevone and Tregudda are the famous 'marble cliffs' where a remarkable stratification of slate and shale may be seen running horizontally along the cliff face. There are deep caves here, and also a 'roundhole' in the field just north of Trevone, close to a gigantic natural arch known as Porthmissen Bridge. These 'roundholes' are formed when the roof of a large cave collapses some way inland, leaving a bit of coast between the hole and the shore, but you will generally find that the sea licks through at high water into the bottom of them by means of the original cave mouth. Seals breed and live in the caves all down this coast, and I have been shocked almost out of my skin by them, as I shall relate later.

Trevose lighthouse and the lifeboat slipway in Mother Ivey's Bay are served by a private toll road with ramps to discourage speeding by wheeled vehicles, but it is worth the effort just to look southward along the sweep of Constantine Bay which is almost always subject to breaking surf.

There follows in near proximity Treyarnon and Porthcothan, both with splendid sandy beaches at low tide, and then comes one of the best-known and certainly one of the finest beauty spots on this north coast — Bedruthan Steps. In springtime the coastal footpath here is a pure delight with riots of gorse, sea-pinks and primroses crowning what must surely be some of the most dramatic coastal scenery in Cornwall. Watergate Bay, with its two miles of golden sands, leads into Porth, Newquay Bay and Fistral Beach, and we are now in the heart of the surfing fraternity. Thousands of holidaymakers are entertained in Newquay every summer watching the malibu surfriders skilfully — and some not so skilfully — doing their acrobatics out there in the swells.

Tad and Sue Ciastula who travelled the globe for ten years sampling the surfing beaches finally settled in Newquay, and have been making and selling boards here for some fifteen years. They run the Vitamin Sea Surf Shop in Crantock Street, and enthused about the sport to me. 'It's a way of life,' says Tad, 'and just about the ultimate form of skill.'

'You've been around the world; what is it that makes Cornwall special so far as surfing is concerned?' I asked him. 'After all, there are beaches everywhere else round the coast of England, why is Cornwall so famous for it?'

'It's just a matter of geography,' he explained. 'The Atlantic storm centres tend to sweep in a vast curve eastward and northward, developing mountainous swells which spread outward from the storm centres. These swells contain enormous energy and form into parallel lines as they move outward . . . and here, right across their path, stretches this peninsula. They heap up as they begin to feel the shallowing seabed, and where you have a very gradually shoaling beach as at Fistral, Watergate, Bude and the like, they change from their deep-water, rounded, sinusoidal form to what is known as a trochoidal shape. This is a sharp-pointed, sometimes almost knife-edged, form. Now, a wave rolling onshore has to break when a critical depth below still-water level is reached. The art is to ride the wave just ahead of the breaking crest, surfing down the steeply inclined leading face then turning to flip back across the crest before you get into too shallow water where the whole wave disintegrates . . . you with it if you're unlucky! It does take real skill and it becomes a way of life. But you have to be young and very fit to get the most out of it,' he added.

Trevaunance Cove, just east of St Agnes Head, used to have a harbour. To be strictly accurate it has in its time had five harbours, but methinks old seadog Neptune must have a personal interest in preserving this delightful cleft in the coastline exactly as it was when Earth cooled down. Five times he has demolished the massive granite sea-wall so carefully and painfully built by Man. If you wish to get some idea of the power in a Cornish storm, potter down to the Cove at low water and take a look at the enormous stone blocks which have been playfully cast about much as a child scatters plastic toy bricks.

Trevaunance, meanwhile, remains much as it always has been. There are interesting disused 'adits' which look like caves in the cliffs here. These were the horizontal entrances to copper and tin mines

Trevaunance Cove, St Agnes in its heyday (above). But Neptune disapproved and to-day (left) you have to search for signs of the old harbour.

which perforate the shore hereabouts, for we are now entering the mining country.

One cannot help marvelling at the ingenuity and sheer courage of those men who, with little more than ropes, blocks and tackle plus a deal of 'know-how', loaded the sailing coasters with mineral ore from the top of those high cliffs. They worked closely with the phases of the moon, grounding the brigs on a falling tide inside the tiny harbour, to be filled and refloated with a subsequent making tide. If the weather changed meanwhile it must have been risky work warping the vessels out and away to the comparative safety of deep water. I know, for I have anchored my yacht *Thyra* close under the bluff where the chutes were rigged just south of the Cove, and there ridden out a south-westerly gale in what at best might be described as a state of enlightened terror, while the seals honked and frolicked at our discomfort in the surf close by and the boat snagged at her anchor chain with more gusto than wisdom.

Oh . . . the swells hereabouts can be marvellous to see, rolling in as they do from the west to thunder in dark green mountains of power against those black cliffs. To enjoy them you have to be ashore, sitting perhaps before a big log fire with a glass of good cheer in the comfortable and characterful Trevaunance Point Hotel on the clifftop.

There are beautiful stretches of sand around Chapel Porth and Porthtowan, but from the unlikely little harbour of Portreath down as far as Godrevy one may see some of the sheerest cliffs on this north coast. In places they almost overhang the sea, with deep caves undercutting. I remember one night we had 'worked the tides wrong' and failed to make St Ives on the ebb, so the flood started pushing *Thyra* back towards Newquay. The wind had fallen away to nothing and darkness was on us, so having a fair weather forecast, and the sea on this occasion being like a millpond, we closed the shore under Deadman Cove and anchored so as to save fuel. Black? My word, under those lowering brows of the land it was darker than Satan's coalcellar. We hoisted our flickering oil-lamp to the mast top as a 'riding light', and stood on deck marvelling at the soft yellow reflections from the dripping cliff face nearby. 'Come on, Ted,' I said, 'get the dinghy off deck and we'll explore, for there will not be a chance like this again in a decade.' It was an optimistic assessment, for the chance hasn't recurred in three decades and probably never will in my lifetime.

Leaving Mu, Ted's wife, in some trepidation at being alone and in sole charge of a forty-foot cutter, we pulled quietly towards the cliffs. I recall the hollow, eerie 'clunk' of our oars in the rowlocks echoing from the sheer rock, while the beam of our hand-torch enabled us to keep a moderately safe lookout. After a while, however, the cliff seemed to recede: the torch beam simply probed into blackness.

Malibu surfing. 'It's a way of life and just about the ultimate form of skill' says Tad Ciastula (opposite, with Sue his wife) who together run the Vitamin Sea Surf Shop at Newquay.

'A cave,' we agreed in whispers, for the whole situation demanded utmost silence in order that all our senses, particularly our ears, could detect any warning lap of water on submerged rocks. The worst that could happen, we reckoned, was that we capsize the small tender, and looking back to the faint and now distant glimmer of our anchor-light, we '. . . thought that maybe we could swim safely enough back aboard?'

It wasn't so much a query, as a bold statement to keep up our spirits. There was something wonderfully atmospheric about it all, and if the King of Prussia himself, somewhat displaced from across the knuckle of the land, had come roaring out at us with a blunderbuss I think we'd both have died instantly of shock. But he didn't, so we nosed carefully into the pitchy void where the inadequate beam of my torch together with the changed quality of the echoes told us that we were in a cavern of some size. 'Stop rowing,' Ted whispered, 'and listen.' I did so, and also switched off my torch just to see whether our eyes unaided could make out the outline of the cave entrance. They could not, and suddenly I realised that we neither of us had the faintest idea of the direction for return. We probed around with the torch again and discussed things, then decided it were best just to listen again in complete silence. There were the faintest sounds of water lapping rock all around . . . just the gentlest, almost indetectable lapping in a silence otherwise so total it made the flesh creep.

How long we sat thus on full alert, I do not know, but what happened next was certainly accentuated by the nature of our situation. There was an earsplitting snort, a splash, and the dinghy gave a massive lurch. 'Ted!' I yelled, certain he was overboard . . . 'Are you . . . ' but Ted's voice came from a foot away. 'A seal . . . quick, the torch.' There were two of them, not ten feet away, their domed heads poking up in alarm, with four reflecting startled eyes looking at us. They seemed enormous, and were breathing mightily as though gathering energy for an assault, the outcome of which in the circumstances was odds against us. But our aquatic brothers and sisters, unlike Mankind who tends to kill anything he doesn't understand, including himself, are not by nature inclined to attack other than their natural prey unless actually threatened. I shone the torch on ourselves so that they might see what it was that had unwittingly disturbed them, for it must have been quite frightening for them to be faced with a single glowing eye.

It proved a good tactic, for they seemed comforted and soon dived, but they did us a good turn, for the clear phosphorescence of their tracks down in the black depths supplied the clue that led back to the cave mouth, and then there was a heartening difference in the air and the nature of sounds, and we knew we were out again.

Above St Agnes. We are entering the mining country now.

It was a somewhat shaky two adventurers who greeted a relieved Mu back aboard, and even to this day I can smell the aroma of grilled liver and onions that wafted towards us from afar as we approached. Of such is the fabric of memories! Happy days, full of adventure and a great freedom; this coast has given much to many that is worth remembering.

We nearly came to grief off Godrevy the next morning. The island with its small lighthouse is barely three cables off the shore, and rather than 'stand off' for some two miles out to sea in order to clear the wretched Stones rocks, I opted to take the inside channel. We were navigating with a very small scale chart of the Bristol Channel which was foolish because it gave insufficient detail close inshore. *Thyra* drew five feet and a sniff or two depending on how many barnacles were hitching a free ride. Suddenly, right in the middle of the narrow channel close ahead, was an unholy disturbance in the water which, to my eye looked remarkably like a submerged reef. It may have been a whale, or Neptune himself come to blow bubbles at these three innocents, but whatever it was it decided us in double-quick time to 'put about' and scutter off to sea where, though time be wasted, boats are safer.

I like St Ives. Strange, isn't it, how just a small act of kindness by one person can set the mood and memories so that when one recalls a place it all seems to glow with goodwill? We had run out of meat on the boat and it was a Sunday. Now we all know it is only when one hasn't got something that one feels the lack of it. We were all of us suddenly very hungry for roast lamb and mint sauce! 'Got it!' I exclaimed to Ted with inspiration. 'We'll go and see if we can buy a leg of lamb from that thumping great hotel overlooking the sea: they're sure to have a refrigeratorfull. They might even have some fresh mint as well.' So it was that Ted and I rowed ashore and eventually presented ourselves, smart and honest as we could appear, to the manager. He listened to our request, then went to one of the splendid lounge windows from where he could see *Thyra* snug at anchor, albeit perishing small on the great green ocean.

'Is that you?' he asked.

'It is.'

'Where have you come from?'

'Swansea . . . and other places.'

'How did you get up here to the hotel?'

'We landed on a rock and came up through . . . oh! Sorry, expect we were trespassing?'

'You were.'

He turned and walked from the room. Suddenly we were thinking it might not have been such a good idea after all, but after a few moments a well-fed gentleman in a white apron appeared bearing both a shoulder and a leg of lamb. 'With the compliments of the manager,' he grinned. 'Oh, look, we've got to pay for this,' we stammered. But it was no use. We returned aboard with enough free meat to keep us bleating happily for a week and, in the circumstances, we agreed to overlook the mint sauce.

Blessings on your head, manager sir, wherever and whoever you may be. I like St Ives.

Godrevy lighthouse: vessels are ill-advised to tackle the narrow channel between the isle and the shore!

Left: Bedruthan at high tide. One of the finest panoramas on this north coast, with the coastal footpath (above) — a wonderful place to be young.

III
St Ives to Land's End

Russell Pascoe (right) shares a yarn with Peter Keeling at Geevor Mine.

As you probe westward along the northern shore of this arthritic knuckle down through Zennor, Morvah, Pendeen and St Just, you walk on virgin rock. Most of it is granite for it is hereabouts that the bones of Cornwall discard their thin flesh of soil to bare themselves entirely to the elements. You may imagine the rock to be solid, and so it is for the most part, but just here you would be mistaken, for Cornishmen have been burrowing underfoot for centuries. In fact, around the area of Botallack Head and the Crowns, this 'solid' rock more resembles a Gruyère cheese so tunnelled is it for minerals.

The Crowns Mine, near Pendeen so dramatically sited on the very last fangs of the land, must have been truly difficult to work, for in its day the ore had to be drawn up to the smelting house at the top of the cliff by pony and cart. The picturesque mine buildings down at the sea's edge were in danger of total dereliction by the end of 1983, but thankfully an alert group, aware of the fact that a rich piece of Cornish heritage was about to disappear forever, set about raising enough cash by public subscription to start the difficult and expensive process of preservation. In 1985 it is good to see that extensive work is already in hand. The engine house of the mine is festooned with scaffolding and one marvels at the skill with which modern construction engineers have managed to erect safe platforms from which to re-point the eroded stonework without the complete fabric plummetting into the chasms far below.

There are four mines still producing tin in Cornwall at this time: Geevor, Wheal Concord, South Crofty and Wheal Jane. The workings of Geevor, based on the old mines of Wheal Stannack and North Levant, now extend for more than two square miles around the main Victory shaft and embrace the Levant mine workings which are largely under the sea itself. The shafts now reach a depth of over 2,000 feet, and if you don't suffer from claustrophobia and fancy sampling the world of a mole, you may, by arrangment only, go down underground.

Join me in so doing. But before we plummet I must tell you that the 'flash' unit on my camera recently did battle with a Cornish cliff, and lost. Now, one cannot take photographs deep underground without a 'flash' and it was here that my friend Peter Keeling came to the rescue. Peter had just bought a wondrously expensive, automatic and computerised camera with a built-in 'flash' and a brain of its own which was quite frightening.

'Peter,' I said over the phone, 'how would you like to come down Geevor mine and see them getting the tin out?'

'Great,' he responded.

'It would be a good chance to test that camera, too,' I added as though by way of an afterthought.

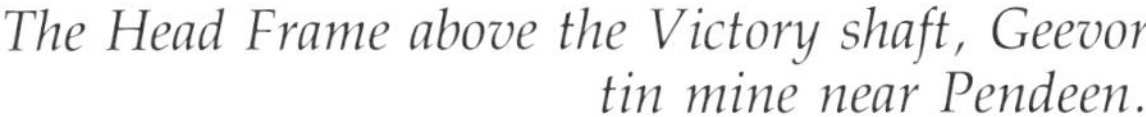
The Head Frame above the Victory shaft, Geevor tin mine near Pendeen.

Look southward from the Avarack and you may see the blue Atlantic flushed red with stain from the ore, as though still bleeding from the memory of that disaster.

'Even greater.'

So it was that the two of us stood, one March morning, gazing up at the vast head-frame which towers above the Victory shaft, and looking around the enormous complex which clutters the clifftops hereabouts. Peter was festooned with electronic equipment; I had my portable tape recorder, and both of us – so we thought – were ready for anything.

Even so, we were taken off-balance by Mr Russell Pascoe, in whose veins I'm sure the ochre mineral itself runs in lieu of blood. It was into Russell's capable hands that the management had wisely placed our innocent souls.

After fitting us out with miner's helmets complete with lamps, and girding us about with webbing belts which secured portable battery-boxes, he forthwith propelled us into the 'cage' which promptly fell – I use the word literally – some fifteen hundred feet into the bowels of the granite.

He plied us meanwhile with vital subterranean facts and, what is more, kept us on full alert by testing us on our ability to comprehend them all. Indeed Russell is an artist of no mean stature, for, in less time than it takes to say 'Botallack', he had reduced my opinion of my own intelligence to match that of a congenital idiot. Some twenty minutes after lurching from the 'cage', a mere stone's-throw from Hell at the bottom of the shaft, encased in protective clothing and sweating like a pig from traipsing the labyrinthine tunnels, and up to my fetlocks in slush, he halts, turns to me and asks: 'Now, you've had a good look at the model of the mine in the office. I've explained the directional planes of the "lodes" where the tin lies in relation to the coastline . . . so tell me, in what direction are we walking now? North, south, east or west?'

A cat in a spin-dryer would have had more clues than I, but you don't display brainlessness to Russell lightly.

'South,' I gasped. It was only three-to-one against.

His expression alone was enough. Turning, wordless, on his heels he splashed on between the narrow-gauge "tram" rails down the six-foot wide, seven-foot high tunnel, and I knew from the set of his shoulders I'd been wrong. But artists are never destructive. Russell builds up your self-confidence again gently and kindly as you edge past roaring compressors, hissing flexible air-tubes, compressed-air driven fans, and mighty-bicepped, flashing eyed Cornishmen doing unprintable things with earsplitting pneumatic drills to the groaning granite, following the 'lodes' of brown tin oxide into the very heart of mother Earth.

Every now and then he would press us back firmly against the dripping walls as a small electric 'tram' with its convoy of swivelling ore-carts clattered past. Far away, above the stacatto rattle of drills and the hiss of escaping air we could hear altogether more bowelshaking roarings as though Earth herself had tummy ache. But it was only the 'grizzley' – a sort of enormous sieve through which the ore-carts were tipped. Ton upon ton of the ore crashed down

The Crown mine near Pendeen. It is good to see that this part of our heritage is being preserved for generations to come.

through the bars into an apparently bottomless pit. This did in fact end at an even more subterranean skip-loading station from which some 700 tons of ore are brought to the surface daily. If the Fiend Himself, hooves horns and all, had winked up at us from down there, it would in those circumstances have passed unremarked!

We pulled ourselves up iron-runged ladders to narrower crevasses, and absorbed infinite mining know-how from chalked diagrams which Russell painstakingly drew on suitable flat granite faces, and it was all quite absorbing except . . . except that I am very sensitive to vibrations.

Not vibrations from quaking granite alone, you understand, but also those more rarefied impulses given off occasionally by human beings in extremity. It was sometime while clambering over great newly-dislodged blocks of glittering rock, wet with mineral-rich water which dripped from the roof, our hands thick with cassiterite-laden mud, that I began receiving them all down my spine from behind. Back there, Peter was caressing his camera like a mother would a newborn babe. 'It's the lenses,' he shrieked above the din, dislodging a lump of mud from the viewfinder with what he thought was a smile. 'They're smoking up with the humidity . . . and I think there's

Edward Harris at the controls of the cables which raise and lower the 'cages' at Geevor tin mine.

something wrong with the shutter mechanism, it's short-circuiting.'

'Have you got any photos at all?' I bellowed.

'A whole reel but my guess is half of them will be fogged-up, and I'm NOT opening it to re-load. I'm just trying to keep the thing in one piece and I hope for your sake,' he added with what I thought was great lack of compassion for my feelings, 'that the damn thing isn't wrecked!'

By the time we were crammed with Russell into yet another 'cage' – this time one whose floor tilted at an odd angle and which seemed to slide unnervingly sideways as we accelerated upwards – there was a distinct 'atmosphere' which had nothing to do with mining tin.

Once back in God-given sunlight we examined the delicate but suffering instrument, and I then made the discovery that my tape-recorder with which I had hoped to get authentic sounds for a 'Down the Mine' programme I was dreaming up, had also gasped to an 'ore-inspired' halt just three minutes after meeting Russell.

Well, you can't win them all, and in the circumstances I think Peter and the camera did pretty well, as you can see. Meanwhile, there was Russell looking at us as though he knew there was one born every minute – and there is. But I tell you this; I wouldn't go down there for a million pounds without him, or his like!

Between April and October you may pay a visit to

About 1500 feet down, Brian Frost and a colleague tip a 'tram' of ore into the 'Grizzley'.

Cape Cornwall, the only cape on Cornwall's rugged coastline, with the offlying Brisons Rocks to the left. The 'chimney' on the cape is in fact an air-vent to a disused mine shaft.

the splendid museum there at Geevor near Pendeen, and very worthwhile it is. In fact it was the old Levant mine nearby which, long ago, was breached by the sea with tragic loss of life. Not surprisingly, for it is said that the miners worked there a mere twenty feet under the seabed and would listen to the boulders rolling back and forth overhead when the storms raged! Today, if you look southward toward Trewellard Zawn from the Avarack you may see the blue Atlantic flushed red with stain from the ore, as though still bleeding from the memory of that disaster.

Truly, this is an elemental bit of coast; enough to give you the shivers when the gales are raging in winter. Gaze inland then, and the lonely chimneys of disused mines seem to point like admonitory fingers to the cloud-shredded sky, as though warning Man not to delve too promiscuously into the body of the land. Sometimes mother Earth takes her revenge!

But we are nearing the end of that land. Walk the clifftops south of Cape Cornwall – the only Cape on Cornwall's rugged coastline and where, incidentally, there is a fine example of a raised beach – and you can feel the ocean encroaching. Indeed it has already separated the Brisons from the main limb of the land to form a terrible hazard for unwary seamen.

It was on those rocks during a storm some hundred years ago that the ill-fated brig *New Commerce* ran

A study in lichen . . . even the rocks at the 'End of the Earth' nourish their own stark flora.

Pedn an Laaz — End of the Earth — or Lands End. From here nothing remains of Cornwall save the lonely stack of Longships Lighthouse on Carn Bras rocks, leading the eye on to the sunken land of Lyonesse.

'. . . no'wt but the short stout mole 'twixt me and smotheration as the swells roared over Cowloe rocks and the sea-wall.' Lugworm *drawn up the slipway among the fishing boats at Sennen Cove.*

aground. All nine of her crew, including the Captain and his wife, managed to get onto that tiny islet but, before the eyes of helpless watchers on the mainland they succombed to the cold and one by one were washed away. All, that is, save one mulatto who managed to keep afloat on a baulk of timber until rescued, half dead, by Sennen fishermen. The Captain and his wife managed to get to the Little Brisons rock where they clung for a whole day. As darkness fell they were still visible from shore desperately clinging there together. A rocket-line was at last got across to them and the woman pulled to dry land. But alas, she died even as she reached safety. Her husband, knowing nothing of his personal tragedy was later brought ashore safely, but went completely out of his mind when told of his loss. The sea demands inexorable payment for human errors.

Sennen is the first and last refuge for a mariner when working up or down this coast, and a very good one it is, though marvellously small. The locals are mostly fishermen and fine seamen and will lend a willing hand when needed, as I know, for I have laid snug here for days in my dinghy *Lugworm* while on passage to the Scillies. Often, as the tide rose there was no'wt but the short stout mole 'twixt me and smotheration as the swells roared over the Cowloe Rocks just off the lifeboat slipway there in the tiny harbour.

So we continue westward, finally to pass the first and last house and drop down beyond the hotel to Dr Johnson's Head. From there nothing remains of Cornwall save the lonely stack of the Longships lighthouse out on Carn Bras rocks, warning mariners from the world over to give a wide berth to this outstretched granite finger; Bolerium of the ancients.

Much has been written of the Land's End, 'Pedn an

Laaz' – (End of the Earth) – of the Cornish. Many, many thousands of feet tread that promontory every summer. But to view it at its elemental best you really have to be afloat – detached as it were – surveying it from afar and perhaps from the crest of a mountainous swell which often builds up hereabouts. The buttress of those cliffs tower up from the depths of the ocean to frown down at you, insignificant mortal that one is.

Then it is that Cornwall speaks with a stern and powerful voice, fixing in true perspective our microbic stature on the face of this lovely planet which spins in the awesome Universe.

We do well to lend an ear!

Sennen lifeboat slipway. The splendid beach beyond takes the full force of seas rolling in from the Atlantic.

Watergate Bay near Newquay.

Stolen Weekend

Quick . . . out from the dark cliff shadow
Into the light
Where winter sun still warms the bones
And foaming lips of sea once more
Reach up to caress, cleanse and absolve
Our feet.

Daily the equinoctial tides
Have washed the summersoiled strand
Lifting detritus back . . . back . . .
To the rock base.

Then, licking down the dark pools
And the cold wrackstrewn crevasses
Have flushed the summer litter, like our memories
To the deeps.
Leaving this winter strand, virgin, mirror-wet
Raped only by our errant footprints —
Prologue to next season.

Interlude

Put your bikini and a bottle of claret in the basket, my dear – the Chateau Latour will do – for we're off to capture the spirit and essence of Cornwall, since today comes straight from Heaven with a 'high' sitting right over the peninsula.

Only one stipulation: you close your eyes for the next half-hour because we're going to a secret valley and, if everyone finds it – it won't be a secret any longer. Bring the sun-lotion as well as towels because there is a shallow stream gurgling from the uplands which falls in a cascade of spray over a low cliff at the shore. Sometimes, when there is a brisk onshore wind, this cascade reverses itself to lift in a fountain of rainbow-spray that can wash off the salt water after we've swum.

What's that? You don't want to swim! Splendid, you can lollop in the rock pools, but come on, every minute is a minute wasted, for as yet there's no breath of wind and by ten o'clock the sun will be a warm blessing.

The author in the Secret Valley.

Stand here for a moment and look down the valley. Do you smell it, that pineapple scent? It's the gorse. Already the sun is dispelling dew from the carpet of yellow flowers, making the air rise with this delicious aroma. Strange, isn't it, how evocative smells can be. I always associate this particular scent, and that of crushed samphire, with a sense of well-being, happiness and freedom. It's simply because I have spent more hours than I care to count down there where this valley capitulates to the sea. Below us, a little farther down, is a level, grass-carpeted ledge hidden in the gorse, large enough for two to spread out with a picnic basket, sandwiches and a good book. Room to stretch out and listen to the silence, far from the hubbub that normally batters our senses into numbness . . . gently now, try not to bounce the basket too much, there's sediment in that bottle!

Put the Latour in that rabbit-hole where it will remain nicely at valley temperature, and the rest of the picnic things in the shade of a gorse bush. Spread out the rug, and we might as well start the day with a liberal application of sun-lotion. The sediment will have settled by then and we can have a small aperitif – oh St Piran! Did you remember the corkscrew?

Good girl. Now, let's just begin to soak it all in with the increasing heat. Soon there will be the faintest wind off the sea as the land warms up, and my guess is that by noon we shall both be ready for a plunge – sorry, a lollop – but first, the aperitif?

You couldn't better it if you were in the Bahamas or Tahiti. In fact we're 'one up' on those over-glamourised spots because we've no snakes nor insects to really plague us, and I firmly believe nowhere on Earth save Cornwall has this uniquely stimulating air that comes from a thousand miles of clear ocean. Look down the valley; do you see that misty, faint, dark-blue line of the sea? The sky just above it is pearl-white, gradually blending to the palest blue until directly above us – look – it's already pure cobalt. Have another sip.

A gull glides down the valley, gracefully without wing-motion, just a quick sideways glance to 'check out' these two intruders. But there is nothing to worry about there so it sweeps on in silence as though it, too, were loath to disturb the magic.

Total silence. Or is it? Have you ever played the game of 'counting sounds'? Just lie quietly, breathing deeply but easily, and actually *listen*. How many sounds can we tot up? There's the sea on the shore down there; that's one. Somewhere very far off a tractor is working . . . just the edge of its engine; that's two. Ah, did you get that? A blackback called from down on the beach; three.

Nothing else? You think that's all? *Listen*. There's the almost inaudible voice of the stream quietly chuckling below. Now and then comes the faintest rustle of grass and gorse in a moving current of air. Suddenly the call of a lark, almost bursting with happy song to greet the warmth, and every now and then the plaintive 'meow' of a buzzard.

Fashions may change (opposite), but the magic of the sea remains the same.

Nearby, too, things are happening. With the increasing heat a whole world of life is waking in the undergrowth. A honeybee drones busily about sampling the rich yellow blossoms on the gorse. Put your ear gently to the ground – you can almost hear the roots spreading and the young shoots growing; the nearly imperceptible crackling of splitting husks down here in the grass forests. There's an ant – elephant size – under my nose, carrying an astonished and evidently paralysed fly purposefully but laboriously off . . . to where? How many ant-miles of intractible jungle will you conquer before proudly presenting your 'kill' to the nest?

Fill up the glass.

There's a soft wind now, as the day gets into gear, and it's going to be a real scorcher: let's turn over otherwise lobsters won't be in it! Talking of lobsters – which we were not – have you ever hunted crabs down there in the rock pools? It's magic. Go at dead low water spring tides when the sea is calm, and you can then explore dark, hidden pools and grottoes that are rarely uncovered. It's another world. You'll not catch any crabs, or if you do they'll be so small it's worse than baby-snatching, but while you're hunting you will begin to appreciate the miracle of form and colour and movement underwater. Great brown-green spatulate leaves of kelp anchored to the rocks by leathery stalks. Translucent filmy green fronds waving with the almost indetectible pulse of the ocean. Millions of tiny barnacles, blood-red sea anemones and . . . ah! A quick dart of movement as a transparent-bodied mite of a fish scuttles away from your shadow.

Gosh, but it's hot. I'm going for a quick plunge.

Icy-cold, the deep water here off the farthest rocks. But just perfect for diving. I strike back towards the beach, vaguely aware of blue-black depths underneath. Do you think there are any 'bluenose' sharks down there? Statistically, of course, it's ridiculously small odds, but I don't feel much like a statistic splashing along here – just vulnerable!

Come on: sandwiches and the last of the wine while we dry off in the midday sun. And sleep? It will be late afternoon when we wake – time for a Cornish cream tea.

Ah yes; I can think of worse ways of spending a day.

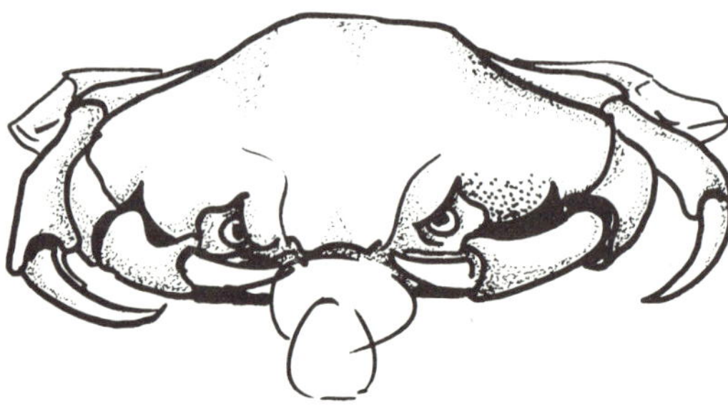

Have you ever hunted crabs down there in the rock-pools? It's magic!

Our breath went through our fingers on that February morn
as we watched her from the headland driving shoreward in the storm.

She lost her masts off Gulland. We thought her gone — and deep —
but wind 'gainst tide just inched her in.
Wife, why do you weep?

She drove in on Tregudda as the light began to fail.
Then she split — and spilled her cargo.

And Dead Men Tell No Tales!

IV
Land's End to Lizard

Places tend to mould the character of people. Similarly a place will magnetize to itself those who are responsive from much farther afield – like to like as it were – and this rugged extremity of West Penwith has an astringent quality that appeals to the iron in the soul of a certain sort of mankind. Our softer accretions wilt and die here on the exposed end of Cornwall. The host body then either flees in discomfort or sends down roots to draw nutrition from the reality of it. Some of them make a distinct mark on history.

Sadly, virtually no early Cornish literature now remains, chiefly due to a deliberate policy of King Athelstan who, in 936 AD, set about eradicating Cornish culture. It is a pity; the peculiar quality of which I speak would have been a valuable ingredient in Britain's total cultural heritage. But like responds to like, and around the turn of the century a quite remarkable coalescence of genius took place in the field of visual art here, between Land's End and the Lizard, most particularly in the environs of Newlyn. At this time there occurred a gathering of painters of unique capacity and stature.

Stanhope Forbes was not the first, for Walter Langley, Edwin Harris and others preceded him, but it was around the personality of Forbes that those of like fibre collected at Newlyn in the late 1800s. Among these were F.W. Bourdillon, Norman Garstin, and Elizabeth Armstrong whom Forbes later married. The attraction they had felt has been attributed to one particular aspect of this coastline – the light. Forbes had already discovered something of its quality while painting in Brittany, but it was here in West Cornwall that there was added another dimension which shines through his work and that of his colleagues.

Analysing this, the conclusion has been reached that these painters, virtually for the first time in the history of art here in Europe, took their easels out into the open air, 'on site' as it were, instead of tucking themselves away in studios reeking of turpentine and oils, and drawing largely on their imagination with its cargo of preconceived ideas as to what things should look like, rather than what in fact they *did* look like. The appellation 'plein air' came to be used for the technique in Brittany and was later applied to those who practised it here.

But I suggest there was more to it than that. I believe they were responding to other subtle influences, not least of which is a certain quality in our Cornish winds. Norman Garstin, one of the more famous of the 'Newlyn School' once wryly commented on this open-air technique: '. . . you can't really be good unless you've caught a cold doing it!' Although intended as a joke, there is in that remark much of the essence of the matter, and I defy any true artist to set up his or her easel on a wet and windy Cornish beach without experiencing and therefore conveying in the finished work something of that astringent, almost antiseptic purity of the air here. It is this which is responsible for the clarity of the light. It may be you are not aware of it until you depart from Cornwall and live elsewhere for a year or two. Then you will detect it as you return, for it is as

Rosemary Ziar, whose work is gaining increasing acclaim.

though each mile westward were a sieve, filtering out the over-rich adornments of the softer and more verdant counties . . . peeling away the overlay of our sensory comforts until there is left only this glitter-sharp, light-quick quality of sea-washed granite, salty and spiced with its own unique flavour of wrack. To me this seems to be the magical quality which artists painting in the area, both then and now, have caught. Study Stanhope Forbes's *Fish Sale on a Cornish Beach* or Lamorna Birch's *Morning Fills the Bowl* and you will catch it. Dame Laura Knight in her highly perceptive study *The Beach* has also caught the quality, though in a gentle and more subdued form, and that incomparable work *The Herring Season* by Charles Simpson is a wonderful example. It is almost as though the subjects were still wet from Creation, responding with a refractive as well as reflective quality.

This is a Cornish experience, and applies not only in the field of detailed observation. There are other realms of perception open to the creative artist. In this field Cornwall spawns some refreshingly original visionaries. One such is the prolific contemporary painter Rosemary Ziar, Cornish born and bred, whose work is gaining increasing acclaim. Her scenario is the human imagination, for when she paints legends it is not just their bones she captures, but rather the underlying almost Shamanistic visions that the myths conjure up. Her studio in Queen Square, Penzance, is an Aladdin's cave of colour and bold originality. She paints competently and fast, almost as if the execution were running in harness with the mercurial quality of the inspiration.

'I'm spontaneous,' she will tell you. 'Oh, maybe while I'm gardening I will think about a legend and let its atmosphere soak in: not the history or geography of it you understand, but simply the way it 'feels' to me, so that when I put the brush to paper I know exactly what it is I'm after.'

She gets it, too. In a refreshingly vivid and playful form she captures the romance and fun of being alive: 'Romanesque' she calls her style. To illustrate how her mind interprets what the lens of my camera slavishly records, compare her painting overleaf of Crown mine under Botallack cliffs with the photograph on page 45. Another example is her large surrealist watercolour *Cornish Heritage* which depicts St Piran's arrival in Cornwall with his message of Christianity.

'What's the Bishop doing lying spread-eagled down there on the rocks?' I asked, somewhat diffidently.

'Oh, him,' she replied in her delightful Cornish burr, 'well, you must remember that here in Cornwall

'A Fish Sale on a Cornish Beach' by Stanhope Forbes. This painting is in the collections of the Plymouth City Museum and Art Gallery.

we have a legacy of smuggling and shipwrecking which walks hand-in-hand with deeply held religious convictions, so when you look at the picture this dual personality must be borne in mind. The Bishop is symbolic of the Church aghast at the primitive flares – used to light the path of the Saint – turning into wreckers' lights, and the welcoming hands into those of avarice. Contrast this with the fishermen in monkish garb who are the forebears of our lifeboatmen risking their lives without thought of reward or for their own safety. Oh, I know St Piran was supposed to have landed at Hayle, but then he was also supposed to have drifted ashore at Perranporth and Perranzabuloe and pretty well everywhere else on our tin-filled coast. Anyway,' she added almost affectionately, 'I think he looks splendid among our craggy Cornish rocks, don't you?'

I had to agree. If you're making history, especially mythical history, then why not make it with panache and imagination?

'And look here!' I exclaimed admiringly, while studying a lively and hauntingly Irish picture of St Ia floating across on her cabbage leaf . . . 'What are all these butterflies?'

'Well . . . cabbage leaves.' She eyed me reproachfully. 'They're very beautiful it's true, all blues and greens, and in the morning dewspangled silver, but, if yours are like mine, they're riddled with holes from caterpillars. And what do these caterpillars turn into? Why – cabbage white butterflies. I simply gave her an attendant chorus of cabbage whites, like our fishing boats coming back with their chorus of herring gulls, that's all.'

All it may have been, but it was a quite fascinating 'all' and the real world seemed utterly prosaic when I left the enchantment of her studio and set about negotiating the reality of Penzance streets!

From the world of art and creative imagination to a world of commerce and creative practical survival. Pass the magnificent fairy-tale edifice of the Mount – about which so much has been written that I refuse to add one unnecessary word – stagger over Cudden Point and round Prussia Cove, then lope along Praa sands and likely as not you will collapse into Porthleven harbour . . . which would be a pity, for this bright and lively little haven deserves a more fitting arrival on your part. Porthleven is unique in one important respect, for it boasts being host to the Curnow Shipping Company, the only deep-sea shipping company to operate today from Cornwall.

'Cornish Heritage' by Rosemary Ziar.

'Crown Mine near Pendeen' by Rosemary Ziar.

You will find no grand chromium-plated skyscraper office block however, just a modest blue and white two-storey building close beside the picturesque harbour, with an outside 'ship's gangway' leading up to the main door. When I bumbled in, her Managing Director, Andrew Bell, was up to the Plimsoll Line (salt water) in negotiation with some antipodean industrialist so I drank a cup of coffee kindly supplied by one of his secretaries, and while so doing was able to study scale models and line-drawings of their ships, together with photographs of far-flung harbours with which they trade. It was not long before, soaking in the sounds and atmosphere of the place, I came to realise that this unassuming complex is, in fact, the nerve centre of a very active and refreshingly vital world-wide trading organisation.

Andrew Bell, fifty years old, stocky, tanned and relaxed with sparse hair and a seaman's eyes, soon disengaged himself from the telex and telephones, to talk with me happily and competently about his company. 'We started' he told me, 'some ten years ago carrying china clay in a traditional 700 ton coaster but, with the onset of the world recession in the early seventies, we began to "shop around" and use the small ships we either owned or managed to freight other cargoes. We first used these ships to carry building materials to Nigeria, and they proved to have one big advantage over our competitors. There was colossal port congestion out there and our five ships – all quite small – could put into tiny ports, rather like Porthleven here. There they could discharge quickly and return, while the large ocean-goers were still waiting for a berth in the main port. So we got a name and established a track record. Our small ships had advantages in other areas too. For instance in 1982 we had management of the first British ship to voyage some 700 miles up the Paraguay River in South America to discharge her cargo at Asuncion. That was a good example of the way a small ship which would not normally be sent on a 6,000 mile ocean voyage was really the ideal vessel, because she could do the job at the other end whereas ocean-goers would have to discharge into smaller river boats or land transport, which adds enormously to the customer's bill.

The St Helena *undergoing trials at Falmouth before leaving for the Falklands. Note the helipad at her stern. Pendennis Castle forms the backdrop.*

'Our ship the *St Helena* was commandeered for the Falklands war and drastically modified for that event, and to put it mildly,' he reminisced, 'that Falklands experience was a bit disturbing. First there was the rather unnerving sight of one's ship being almost taken to bits and re-assembled in the form of a Royal Fleet Auxiliary and then, manned by our crew and having sailed to the war area . . . well, here we were just sitting at home keeping a ghastly rota-list of just *who* was going to ring up *whom* and say: '. . . look, we're terribly sorry but she's been hit by an Exocet missile and there's nothing left.' Mind you the ship took so much tomato sauce to those islands that had she suffered a direct hit the 'Argies' would have broadcast that the entire British Falkland forces had been exterminated! But to be serious again, I can tell you there were those who left here as boys and came back as men, so to speak.'

'Tell me about St Helena, the ship and the island,' I prompted.

'We operate what is virtually a tram-track down there and back. As you may know, the island is in latitude 16 degrees south and 1,000 miles from the nearest land. We run six voyages a year on that route carrying some 2,500 passengers and 25,000 tons of cargo, the technical administration for which all takes place here from this office.'

'What do you bring back from the island?'

'More and more fish, I'm glad to say. What is even better is that the Overseas Development Administration have just now got a Cornish fisherman from St Ives out there showing the islanders how to catch lobsters! Believe me, at the price lobster meat is fetching on the international market, the St Helenans are doing very nicely out of it.'

'And the future of Curnow Shipping Company?' I asked. Andrew thumbed through a large photo album and stopped at the picture of a most ungainly looking ship, packed to the davits with cargo. 'Catamarans,' he said. 'You're looking at the ship of the future. They're cheaper to build and compared with a conventional deep-draught vessel they are far more cost-effective to operate.'

'Do you propose taking any into your fleet?'

Andrew Bell, Managing Director of the Curnow Shipping Company, with Porthleven harbour in the background.

'If they do the job more effectively, and that means more safely and more cheaply for the customer and us, we shall use them,' he grinned. 'It's why we're successfully in business.'

We have ranged a long way out into the world from this Coastline of Cornwall, I reflected as I focused my camera on Andrew, with Porthleven harbour in the background. But then, I mused, one way and another Cornwall has had – and still has – quite an impact on the rest of the world.

''Em, he snorted, his beard bristling with indignation, 'ef I 'ad my way I'd 'aive 'em oal awver en t'say!' He waved his stick toward the riot of caravans in the distance – I'm not saying where – and I must agree he had a point. They are, in the opinion of many, the bane of Cornwall. In my own opinion this has an element of truth in it, but is largely due to unsuitable siting and the general air of untidiness which many 'sites' convey. Colour is one of the affronts: if legislation were passed that every caravan permanently sited here, or temporarily entering Cornwall, had to be coloured deep moss-green which would blend with the countryside it might help matters. Come to think of it, there could be money for some Cornish firm supplying transfers of blackthorn blossom, or sea-pinks to stick on their sides for camouflage! Some of them are so garish they stick out like a sore thumb, often on the crest of a hill or clifftop. Some of them are a blot on the landscape.

To be fair, that is only half the equation. But for caravans, many thousands of people would not be able to enjoy the type of holiday they want on this peninsula. I myself, many years ago, lived happily and memorably for a short while in a caravan here; but I do recall it was sited in a small private valley hedged about with trees and completely out of sight of any public highway or footpath. It suited me fine, for I've never been very keen on estate-living, whether in caravans or houses. Another point which has to be borne in mind: a field full of caravans can represent better economics than a field full of potatoes. They're a good 'crop', as are the car parks which have taken over areas of this coastline. Privately owned or Council run, they both bring in a sizeable income annually, so let's not be inflexible about the problem. The answer is responsible attitudes and wisely enforced controls. Which is where the National Trust is a boon, and on this west-facing shore south of Porthleven much of the coastline is their property.

Loe Bar and the pool itself are bounded by Trust property, and very beautiful that great freshwater lake is, fed by the River Cober. The river runs through the western end of Helston a bit inland, and since the Bar was formed by the wash of the sea a long time ago, problems arose. The Cober filled the Loe and Carminows Creek, both of which kept on rising slowly. Helston was likely to get wet feet, so a short tunnel had to be burrowed through the cliff on the north side of the Bar, to allow the water to flow

St Michael's Mount. A marriage of myth and history.

seawards and keep the level controlled. It solved the problem all right, so long as the wash of the sea didn't fill the tunnel-end with the sandy shingle of the Bar. Every now and then it has to be cleared.

There are trout to be caught in the fresh water, but only if you have a licence to fish, and thank heaven there are no roads actually running along the banks of the pool, so it remains a wonderfully unspoilt place. The car park to the south is some distance from Loe Bar, and the farm track which leads down to the sea has its own attractions in the hedgerows, as I found, being a riot of wild campion, bluebells, foxgloves and dog-rose.

It is a grand bit of coast to walk, down to Church Cove south of Gunwalloe, and on round to the popular Mullion Cove which does, I suppose, get a bit of a lee from the Island just to seaward. It needs it. In winter I have seen the sea thundering over that harbour wall as though it were bound for Porth Mellin, if not Mullion village. The whole of this area is fully exposed to the prevailing south-westerly winds, and it can be awe-inspiring to watch when Neptune is playing squash with his Kingdom, using this Lizard Peninsula as his front wall.

Speaking of the Lizard, we are approaching latitude 49 degrees 57.5 minutes north, and are you aware this is a noteworthy moment? We have rounded the most westerly headland in the whole of England, and now just beyond Kynance Cove is the most southerly – Lizard Point. It is a massive promontory, vying with Land's End in grandeur, and in one sense at least excelling it, for it supports our premier lighthouse.

Over one hundred years ago a Mrs Craik, who wrote under the pseudonym of Dinah Maria Mulock, in her book *An Unsentimental Journey through Cornwall*, recounts how one evening at sunset in a small boat off Kynance Cove, she was asked by the boatman to 'look out for the Lizard Lights'. 'And sure enough,' she continues, 'the instant the sun's last spark was quenched in the sea, into which he dropped like a red round ball, out burst two substitute suns, and very fair substitutes too, making the poor little moon in the east of no importance whatever. The gleam of them extended far out upon the darkening ocean, and we could easily believe that their light was equal to 20,000 candles, and that they were seen out at sea to a distance of twenty, some say thirty, miles.'

'Except in fog, and the fogs at the Lizard are very bad. Then you can see nothing, not even the lights, but they keep sounding the foghorn every minute or so. It works by the same machinery as works the Lights – a big steam engine; you can hear it bum-bumming now, if you listen,' added the boatman.

And so you could in those days, I have no doubt. It is worth bearing in mind as you approach the Point that there has been a lighthouse – though, alas, not always a light – of some sort or another here since Sir John Killigrew lit his own privately run light in 1619. It was a precarious venture, meant to be financed by a

Fish Sale on a Cornish Quay, 1985.

levy from ships passing the Lizard Point. The trouble is that the ships *did* pass, and who knew where they were bound, or what was their name? He financed the project from his own pocket, sure in the knowledge that the Dutch alone had, during the previous decade, lost ships trying to round the Point to a value of some £100,000. That fact alone, he felt certain, would, out of gratitude for the service he provided, guarantee receipt of the levy. It did not. The lighthouse had to close for lack of funds to run it – and it burned an enormous amount of coal on top of the tower, by all accounts. It was not until 1752 that one Thomas Fonnerau obtained permission from Trinity House to erect a second tower, each of the two to show 'good and sufficient fires'.

Which is all a far cry from the one white tower which today sends a single electrically-powered beam of two and a half million candlepower sweeping through some 230 degrees of the horizon every three seconds, and visible for thirty miles on a clear night. You may wonder that the distance that light is visible from ships at sea is akin to that of the earlier coal-fired lights? The reason is that visibility is restricted by the curvature of the earth. The average ship, if beyond thirty miles from the light, is below the horizon! There is no bum-bumming of a steam engine working the light mechanism now; a quiet electric motor rotates four lenses containing in all 364 curved prisms of glass which concentrate the light from two 3,000 watt lamps. The life of each lamp is a mere fifty days, and each costs £240 . . . and the whole unit of four lenses floats in a dish containing half a ton of mercury so as to be almost friction free. The tower, in addition, also transmits a radio signal with the identifying letters 'LZ' in morse code for a distance of some fifty miles, with which ships can fix their position in relation to Lizard Point, even though far beyond visibility range.

Walk round the cliff path beneath the light, and you will see the companion tower built by Fonnerau matching the light tower, but without a light of its own. You will also notice two large black trumpet-like objects mounted atop a small white building: beware! These are twin foghorns, driven by compressed-air,

Mullion Cove on a calm day . . . but I have seen the sea thundering over that harbour wall as though it were bound for Mullion village itself.

A grand bit of coast to walk . . . down to the Church Cove south of Gunwalloe.

and if you should be walking below them in poor visibility when they come into operation you might well leap the 200 odd feet into the sea to escape their blast. To a sailor, becalmed in thick fog, and unsure whether the dreaded 'race' of the tide is taking him onto the fangs of Men Hyr rocks just off the Point it is a dreary and fleshcreeping sound. Today the owners of ships are only too happy to pay their Light Dues, from which Trinity House maintains in immaculate condition all the lighthouses around our coast.

Lizard lighthouse, the most southerly point of our land. Two and a half million candlepower sweeps a powerful finger of light around the horizon every three seconds . . . a far cry from the original coal-fired bonfires of Thomas Fonnerau in 1752. 364 curved prisms of glass (above) float in half a ton of mercury to rotate almost free of friction while focussing the light from two 3000 watt lamps.

V
Lizard to Dodman

With one or two notable exceptions it is my experience that the human race is not much concerned with the preservation or enhancement of its environment. The hard pressures of survival, greed or profit in one form or another, tend to override such considerations as beauty and regard for natural flora and fauna, linked with real appreciation of the miraculous ecological balance which nature has achieved over many millions of years.

So it is heartening to come across the small valley of Poldowrian on this south-facing coast halfway between Cadgwith and Coverack, itself a designated area of outstanding natural beauty. Over the past fifteen years the valley has been lovingly converted by Peter and Valerie Hadley from an unkempt riot of bramble and scrub into one of the most delightful gardens you could wish to find, and of a character wholly in keeping with the natural surroundings.

It is a small jewel in a near perfect setting. Unassuming, without any pretensions of grandeur and subject to the minimum of artificial landscaping, it simply makes the most sensitive and artistic use of the natural features. A small stream chuckles down from a farmstead, and the valley as it deepens gives shelter from the salt winds, and provides natural rock buttresses to supply that essential third dimension of height which so many grander gardens lack. The

Valerie Hadley cuts a bloom from the prolific Camellia Adolphe Audusson in Poldowrian garden. In the right foreground Rhododendron Lady Alice Fitzwilliam scents the air beside a Norway Maple.

Helford River. The contrast here to the bracing and elemental north coast is very marked.

stream, as though elated by its passage through such an enchanted grove, leaps in a final frolic over the cliff to splash the rocky beach 200 feet below.

You may stumble on Poldowrian unawares as I did, while following the coastal footpath. If you do, please remember that although the footpath is public, the cliff land and beaches are private, as of course is the garden on which you look down. If the owners happen to be working there you may be lucky enough to be invited to walk round. Otherwise you will have to wait for one of the Open Days that are held occasionally during the summer: these are advertised locally and the opportunity should not be missed.

As you stand looking southward, you will see on your left that promontory of Lankidden, where even an untrained eye can discern the grass-covered rampart running across the neck of this small peninsula. This was an Iron Age 'cliff castle' similar to others round the Cornish coast such as the Rumps near Portquin. These 'cliff castles' made good natural fortresses, easily defended on the seaward side, while protected by earthworks against assault from landward. Those who occupied and fortified them were almost certainly the Veneti, colonists from the area of what is now Vannes on the west coast of Brittany, and closer to Poldowrian by sea than Taunton is by land. Julius Caesar in his *Gallic War* recounts how the inhabitants of that area, when threatened with attack by his legions, sent for help to their kinsmen in Britain whose practice it was to fortify headlands and always keep their boats close at hand.

It was such visible evidence of prehistoric habitation nearby that first prompted Peter Hadley, himself a keen amateur archaeologist, to look for traces of prehistoric man at Poldowrian, where a sheltered valley and a stream of fresh water must have provided ideal conditions for settlement. It was no surprise, after a cliff fire in 1967, that a system of small irregular fields was revealed, bounded by obviously very ancient low stone walls. A prehistoric dating was confirmed in 1969 by the discovery within them of a Bronze Age round house, eventually excavated in 1980 by the Cornwall Archaeological Society.

Two other important prehistoric sites have also been discovered and excavated at Poldowrian. The first of these, excavated in 1978, yielded many fragments of what is known as 'Beaker' pottery, typical of an imported Bronze Age culture, and radiocarbon dated to 2,100–1,500 BC. More important still is the Mesolithic (Middle Stone Age) site excavated jointly in 1980 by the CAS and the Department of the Environment, where a dating of 4,500 BC was forthcoming from the occupation level. It seems likely, therefore, that Poldowrian was occupied over a very long prehistoric period, and it may even have been farmed continuously for some 3,000 years.

Left: remains of the Bronze Age round house discovered at Poldowrian in 1969. Right: a model reconstruction of the round house by Peter Hadley, on view in his museum.

In order to display the numerous finds, Peter Hadley has converted the upper part of a barn into a most interesting and well laid-out Museum of Prehistory. It is well worth visiting on Open Days – or by appointment for schools and archaeological students – for, apart from the knowledge it imparts, it succeeds in conveying just how recent, geologically speaking, our human species is. Which is all very salutory, for we do tend to consider ourselves Lords of the Earth, if not the Universe . . . though in fact we have been here for the mere blink of an eye when compared with the *4,600 million* years since the birth of our small solar system!

Throughout this journey we have been constantly coming across and using the coastal footpath, and it is a fact that the whole of this western peninsula is traversed by 824 kilometres of path known as the South West Peninsula Coast Path. It runs from Minehead in Somerset to Poole in Dorset and is divided into four sections, of which the Cornish part extends some 430 kilometres from Marsland Mouth, to Cremyll in Plymouth Sound. Rarely does it stray far from the sea, often following well worn Coastguard footpaths, and this splendid concept was originated and brought into effect by what is now known as the Countryside Commission. The Cornish section was officially opened in May 1973, and the path is now carefully maintained using funds from the Commission administered by the local councils across whose areas it runs.

It is certainly a boon for all who love the coast, for it means that when walking the path, and provided we do keep strictly to it, we have legal right of way and are not trespassing. Of course, all such freedoms do call for a reciprocal sense of responsibility on our part. If closed when we get to them, then gates must be left closed. Stiles must be treated with care, and the 'hedges' of stone respected for what they are – barriers to stop animals straying. Not only should we refrain from climbing over, or walking along the tops of them, but we should, where possible, replace obviously dislodged stones to give the farmers a helping hand in what is a difficult task.

Above all, in the heat of summer, extra precaution must be taken to avoid fire. A cigarette end, perhaps quite unconsciously dropped into tinder-dry bracken, will smoulder long enough for the guilty party to walk out of view before one tiny blade of grass bursts into flame – and hundreds of acres of grassland, crops, gorse and scrub may be destroyed without the person responsible even knowing that it was he, or she, who started it. Glass bottles are another cause of fire, for they can focus the sun's rays like a magnifying glass.

Another perennial source of worry to farmers and landowners is pet dogs. I have seen the carnage when, one lovely summer afternoon, twenty bullocks were panicked by a dog which playfully chased them down a sloping field atop the cliffs. Unable to stop at a low 'hedge' they careered headlong across the footpath straight over the cliff edge. Rescue services worked all evening and into the night recovering the few survivors by helicopter, while a Coastguard team

aided by vets helped to put most of the dreadfully injured beasts out of their misery, then had to haul the carcases up the cliff face . . . all for the want of a dog lead!

We, the public, enjoy our freedom to walk this coastline: it is our responsibility to safeguard it. Much of the area traversed by the path is designated as 'Defined Heritage Coast', and as such will be protected and preserved for as long as Man has any appreciation left for his natural, unspoilt environment. The Council for the Protection of Rural England was founded in 1926 with the specific objective of keeping a watchful eye over the development of rural areas, particularly in the field of 'Town and Country Planning'. The CPRE later became a registered charity, and formed county branches of which Cornwall was one of the earliest. The Council now has a national membership of some 30,000 and has the privilege of being consulted by many District and County Councils. Parish Councils and local amenity societies also lend their strength by affiliation. Nationally and locally the CPRE meets with major environmental bodies such as the Countryside Commission and The National Trust, and often represents the national view when parliament has to be lobbied over some important matter.

Nobody who appreciates our heritage can be unaware of, or ungrateful for, The National Trust. Many of the beautiful areas we traverse on the coastal footpath are owned or administered by this very worthwhile organisation which manages to strike a workable, though sometimes delicate, balance between commercial interests and preservation of the land and many of our historic houses.

1985 saw the celebration of *Enterprise Neptune* which was launched in 1965 under the patronage of the Duke of Edinburgh. The object of this enterprise is to raise money in order to either purchase outright, or obtain convenants over, stretches of coastal land as and when these become available. Its motto: '*Don't let it become just a memory*' speaks for itself.

Twenty years ago the Trust conducted a survey which revealed that of the entire coastline of the United Kingdom, only some 900 miles remained in its original unaltered state. All the rest was 'developed' in one way or another – and we know what that means! By raising cash to the sum of £7 million the Trust, which was set up in 1895, has now managed to achieve control over nearly half of those valuable remaining unspoilt areas. More than seventy Trust Wardens keep a close eye on this property, preserving it for use and appreciation by the general public. It is then in safe hands, for once the Trust has acquired the land it cannot be purchased – even compulsorily – without the matter going before a joint committee of both Houses of Parliament. To date there are over a million members, many of whom have donated gifts of land. In Cornwall the National Trust operates from their headquarters in the beautiful Lanhydrock House, near Bodmin.

Over forty years ago, while navigating a badly damaged Landing Craft through those intricate waterways known as the 'sunderbans' between Chittagong and Calcutta, I had the unusual experience of having to negotiate my ship's mast through thick forests of trees which all but joined their foliage overhead. In the foliage, and in great profusion, were nesting flocks of wild flamingoes . . . or they may have been cranes of some sort. Whatever they were, at the approaching 'purr' of the ship's engines they one and all stretched their necks upward in alarm, peering to see what manner of monster was coming to disturb their peace.

I little thought that one tranquil evening the experience would be more-or-less repeated in Cornwall. But so it turned out, though the birds were certainly not flamingoes, and my 'ship' but a modest open boat. My eighteen-foot dinghy *Lugworm* had brought my wife Brenda and myself safely from the Camel estuary on the north coast 'round The Land' to Helford River. As we approached Gillan Creek just south of the river, the wind fell light, so not wishing to disturb the peace of a quiet spring evening with the outboard motor, we took to the oars and rowed gently up the creek.

If you know the Helford and its adjacent waters you will probably agree it is at its best when the trees are in young green leaf, crowding down as they do to overhang the water's edge. Up Gillan Creek they almost join leaves overhead near Carne and Manaccan. In those trees, and in equal confusion, nested scores of herons. Just as at the mouth of the great Ganges river, they one and all craned their necks to look down on us in alarm, and for a moment we both felt weirdly transported to the dreamlike world of *Alice in Wonderland*.

A wonderland it truly is, with an enchantment that has to be experienced. The contrast here to the bracing and elemental north coast is very marked, for now we are approaching perhaps the most pastoral, soporific stretches of Cornwall, embracing the St Just in Roseland peninsula. Here in the Helford River, wooded creeks up to Port Navas, Constantine, Gweek and Mawgan are only fitfully served by occasional winding country lanes, and the small valleys around Rosemullion Head just to the north are thick with trees. It is almost a shock therefore that a mere two miles to the north is Carrick Roads and the entrance to Falmouth harbour, which is already advertising its presence by the ships lying at anchor in the bay.

One might think that a marriage of those qualities which make for a successful holiday resort and the hard commercial world of a large dockyard would appear to conflict, not least one might expect, in the aesthetic, visual field. Somehow Falmouth has managed it, and kept a unique and vital atmosphere of tradition and history alive while so doing. Whether this is the result of responsible and careful planning,

Falmouth panorama from Pendennis Castle.

If you have not yet done so, go up Castle Drive and spend a day exploring Pendennis Castle.

or whether it has just evolved naturally from a chance balance of interests which proved by the geography of the harbour to be compatible, I do not know. The fact is, as all who enjoy the place must agree, that the dockyard forms a splendid backdrop to the town and harbour, and helps to provide an atmosphere quite different from that of any other resort.

You would not think, as you browse through that lovely Queen Mary garden at the southern end of the bay, then walk along the splendid cliff road, backed as it is with the fine hotels and their own gardens, that just over the peninsula huge ocean liners lie in their protected berths, with all the derricks and cranes and paraphernalia of a dockyard. Somewhere in the happy equation, I suspected, the Harbour Commissioners must have a hand, so, seeking to gain some insight as to what it must be like to administer the daily activities of a port with such varying demands, I sought an interview with the Harbour Master.

Captain Banks is fit, tall, lean and tanned with that deep underlying pigmentation which argues long familiarity with tropic suns. He is in fact a Sussex man, ex P & O officer with a Master's Ticket, and after serving here as Deputy Harbour Master took over as Harbour Master in 1978. I asked him how, if at all, the fact that Falmouth combines a commercial port, a dockyard, and a very extensive pleasure boat haven added to his job of administering the aquatic side of the place.

'It certainly gives variety,' he said. 'In the yacht marina at Ponsharden there are, at the moment, berths for 250 craft, and planning application is under way for an extension to take another 150. In addition we have something like 700 moorings for resident craft which are here all the year round, and in a normal season we can also expect to handle about 1,500 visiting boats.' Of course there are many more moorings up at Truro and Penryn, but these don't come under this authority.

'On the commercial side, in 1984 we had 1,650,000 tons of shipping use the port. Some of it comes to the docks, but tankers go up to the wharf just this side of Falmouth marina, while others go down to the quarries. Then there are the floating fish-factories, and various explosive-transhipment vessels. It's a rich diet,' he laughed.

'In administrative time,' I asked, 'what proportion is taken with pleasure boating, as opposed to the commercial activity?' Rather to my surprise he told me that the majority of administration from his office was concerned with the pleasure craft. 'The administration of merchant shipping all takes place in a fairly streamlined manner,' he explained. 'It's well-founded and the result of long experience and a predictable need. Ship Masters know precisely what they require, and we have the documentation to deal with every aspect of this: it's standard throughout the country.

'Pleasure craft are quite different. With them it's a one-to-one basis because you are dealing with a "ship owner" every time and they have very particular needs. On top of all this, of course, we're responsible for the licensing of all the pleasure boats with seating for up to twelve passengers which operate from the harbour, and also the boatmen who run them. I'm talking now of the day trips to the Helford River and up the Fal, which are immensely popular with the visitors.'

Ancient and modern: an oil rig in Falmouth roads awaiting a tow to her operational site, with spritsail barge in the foreground.

'You must be a busy man,' I commented, looking at the enormous red funnel that towered above the cranes behind him, then trying to count the forest of masts at the visitors' yacht haven off the north quay.

'One has to keep a watchful eye on it all,' he smiled, 'but I'm backed up by a very competent and hardworking staff, and that makes it all run smoothly.'

But behind that towering red funnel, a little beyond the cranes and wharves of the compact dockyard area, the amber-coloured stonework of Pendennis Castle on the Point looks down on it all. Henry VIII knew how to site his coastal fortifications in the most dramatic and commanding positions. Even today, as you enjoy a swim or paddle on Castle Beach, or maybe dine in splendour in a window-bay of one of the fine hotels along Cliff Road, there is still a comforting – almost protected – feeling that the castle up there is keeping a benign and watchful eye on things, and ensuring that all is well with the town, the harbour and the visitors.

If you have not yet done so, go up Castle Drive and spend a day exploring those historic buildings. But take with you a copy of Mary and Hal Price's *Castles of Cornwall*, also published by Bossiney, for you may then re-live the turgid background of the place as you tread the well-preserved battlements, climb the circular staircases, and peer from the gun emplacements which have, with their cannons, been so commendably maintained. You will get the finest view of the whole area from the castle roof-top, with the town, Carrick Roads and the Fal River, and the lighthouse on St Anthony Head opposite laid out like a map beneath.

What you may not suspect as you walk aloft, re-living history up here, is that electronic ears and eyes from geostatic satellites far out in space are beaming high-frequency signals to a centre beneath your feet here on the extremity of the Point. This is the South West Region nerve centre of HM Coastguard, central co-ordinating station for some 660,000 square miles of ocean watched over by this worthwhile organisation. Remoter areas such as Trevose Head, St Ives, Pendeen, the Isles of Scilly, Lizard Point and Falmouth itself are all connected directly to this Maritime Rescue Co-ordination Centre. Down there alert officers keep a twenty-four hour watch with the aid of the most up-to-date technology. Their business, which is closely linked to the lifeboat and other rescue services, is to be aware of any potential or actual disasters at sea or on the coast.

To give some idea of the scale of their activities, in 1984 alone the specialist cliff-rescue services in this area were called out 136 times. That year, in the six months between April and September, there were 225 casualties between Tintagel Head and Dodman alone. Lifeboats were launched 103 times, 13 RAF Nimrods and 72 RAF helicopters took to the air, while Coastguard Rescue Teams were called out 138 times. In all, 363 lives were saved, while only nine lives were lost. The co-ordination, control and administration of all this goes on from here in Falmouth.

When I visited the centre and spoke to the various officers, I gradually entered into an entirely different world of instant nation-wide communication, unbelievably extended horizons, and above all a competent, no-nonsense atmosphere of dedicated men whose prime concern was to, if humanly possible, avert disasters. Whether it be little Archie whose head is jammed in a rock-cleft at St Agnes with a rising tide, or Phyllis who is drifting towards America on her death-trap beach inflatable, or maybe just some supertanker foundering off Southern Ireland . . . it's these men and women of the Coastguard Service who first gather all available facts and then swing into action, alerting and keeping informed all the other rescue services.

Porthcuel Creek, wriggling up to Gerrans and St Just is unusual in that it splits the Roseland peninsula neatly in half, longways north and south with the quaint little port of Portscatho on its eastern shore, and that splendid Pendower Beach under the Nare Hotel. Nare Head is tricky when navigating down this coast, for like Dodman Point there is no light to warn of the promontory. The Gull Rocks off the nose of the Nare are worth rounding in a small boat, just for the profusion of seabirds which rise in a discordant and alarming clamour at your approach. I have been literally plastered with good luck from shags and cormorants lumbering down and over my canoe from the ledges above. It was fun.

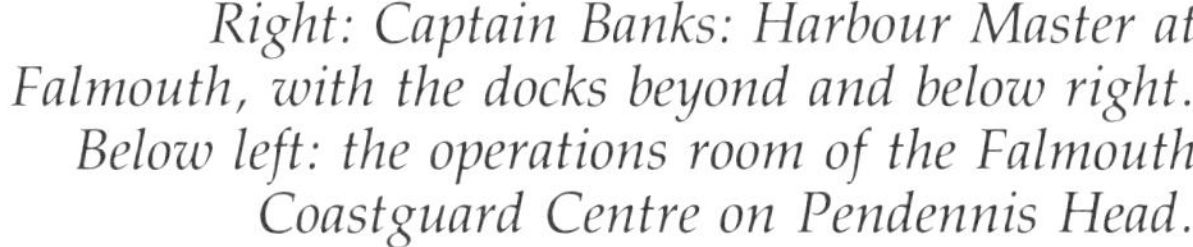

Right: Captain Banks: Harbour Master at Falmouth, with the docks beyond and below right. Below left: the operations room of the Falmouth Coastguard Centre on Pendennis Head.

FY 317
FY 222
FY 386

Left: Mevagissey harbour about 1920. Above: the same view to-day.

So we travel round Veryan Bay, past Portloe and Portholland, which is not a port at all, and Caerhays Castle, exploring the Dodman if we will, sunning ourselves on the lovely stretches of Vault Beach and Great Perhaver Beach near Gorran Haven which is, more or less, a haven, though bloodcurdling for a sailor when the easterly gales rampage. And here is Mevagissey, a major fishing port of Cornwall, with its ever active quays and picturesque waterfront which has changed little enough in the past half century as you can see from the accompanying pictures. But here again it is a rough-and-tumble for the boats to get safe into harbour when those easterlies blow, and the swell bursts over the outer mole completely engulfing the pierhead light!

Summer visitors often have little idea of the real violence of the Cornish seas, though for the more perceptive observer something of it is discernible in those lines etched deep into the seawise faces of the fisherfolk you may chat with in this working harbour.

Left and below: Mevagissey breakwater in storm conditions.

Portmellon in high seas.

VI
Dodman to Rame Head

Two hundred years ago Charlestown as it is now called, did not exist. There was just the tiny hamlet of West Polmear, or West Porthmear, with some nine inhabitants whose main occupation was pilchard fishing. But the adjacent beaches, tucked as they were up in St Austell Bay and protected from westerly winds and swell, proved a convenient spot for bringing boats ashore for loading and unloading cargoes. Even so, this was a risky business, for if the weather changed while the boats were ashore between tides, the difficulty of getting afloat again without damage was very real.

In 1789, Charles Rashleigh, a local gentleman, attorney and landowner, gave some thought to the obvious need for a safe haven, and over the next six years built the harbour, much as we see it today. It became known as Charles' Town, or more simply Charlestown, and housed facilities for shipbuilding, loading and unloading, as well as pilchard fishing which, at that time, was still the main occupation of the area. Local tin and copper mining was in its infancy then, and the tinners used to cement the stones of their furnaces with a clay dug locally. An insignificant fact it might appear to be, but it was the harbinger of great things to come. The clay, which was unique to the area, became extremely hard in the intense heat of the ovens, and in 1796 it was found to be of great benefit as a really hard glaze for chinaware. It became known as 'china clay' and was soon in great demand.

By this time the locality had become rich in copper mines also, there being eighteen working mines in the areas of Crinnis, Biscovey, Tywardreath and St Blazey alone. This ore was also brought down to the harbour for shipment. So Charlestown became a focal point for what was already a somewhat industrialised area. Few, however, could have forecast at the time of that first discovery of 'china clay', the enormous commercial development which has taken place across the last century and a half. By the end of the 1800s the mining of copper and tin had virtually died, but china clay continued to gain in reputation and is now acknowledged as being second-to-none the

Par harbour where most of the china clay loading is now done.

Charlestown harbour remains to-day much as Charles Rashleigh built it some 200 years ago.

world over. One of the main features of this coastline today is the white 'mountains' just a little inland which are the waste material from the clay workings.

So the history of Charlestown is largely a story of commercial development through the changing eras of shipbuilding, pilchards, tin, copper and clay. Although recently much of the shipment of the latter has moved to Par and Fowey just to the east, it is in this Georgian village of Charlestown that you may relive this history in a fascinating way, for in September 1976 a splendid Museum of Industrial and Marine Archaeology – known locally as the Shipwreck Centre – was opened alongside the harbour.

This unique enterprise is largely due to the foresight, enthusiasm and hard work of Richard Larn and Roy Davis, ably helped by their respective wives and Charlestown Estate Limited. The former two are active commercial divers of great experience. It all started when they contributed items which they themselves had recovered from various sunken wrecks, but over the ensuing years their collection has been steadily increased by donations from other sources. It is now a great attraction for visitors, with full–size working representations of life across the centuries as lived by the various craftsmen in the area.

The Shipwreck Museum, which forms a larger part of the display, must be unique, for it has been planned and supervised from the start by these underwater experts. It contains, together with many scores of photographs, mock-ups of very early diving apparatus together with a most realistic tableau of the recovery, through a hole burnt in her hull, of over £40 million worth of gold bullion from HMS *Edinburgh* sunk in the Barents Sea by a German U-Boat in the last war.

Up until the mid 1600s, when disaster struck a ship it was only the *contents* of her holds that was of any import. The identity of the vessel and the fate of her crew were of no consequence. The law of the time decreed that the vessel was not, in fact, a wreck so long as a man or a dog survived, so it must have been a sore temptation for those watching to hope, at least, for there to be no survivors . . . if not to take active measures to ensure that this was the case! This fact has given rise to many a bloodthirsty story of luring ships onto the coast by the placing of false lights, with the added drama of instant despatch for the poor wretches who managed to struggle ashore. It may be there were a few such cases long ago when life was a deal harder than it is now, but I find it hard to believe, for in my experience the nature of Cornishmen, and Cornishwomen, is quite the reverse.

'What was it,' I asked Richard Larn, 'that appealed to you in recovering items from sunken wrecks, and just how was the concept of this Shipwreck Centre born?'

'Roy Davis and I have been diving together for many years,' he told me. 'Behind the Museum concept as you see it now, there are three partners: Charlestown Estate Limited, Roy Davis and myself. Prior to the existence of the Museum, when maritime archaeology was very much in its infancy, we felt that there really ought to be somewhere that interesting

Right: Lantic Bay. A splendid view on the incomparable walk from Polruan to Polperro.

Left: The Rashleigh Inn, Polkerris, to-day. Above: As the waterfront appeared before the original inn, seen above the brig's bowsprit, was demolished. A painting in oils by Michael Kerris. Opposite: Elizabeth Harrower beside the figurehead of the Rashleigh Inn.

items recovered from the sea could be put on display to the public as a whole. To put it bluntly, the major museums of this country are not particularly interested in maritime archaeology, and although the recent raising of the *Mary Rose* has sparked off a certain train of interest, it's still a fact that the major national museums will rarely accept exhibits recovered from wrecks. So, from a very large stockpile of material which Roy and I had collected, we decided to select some and put in on display. This was such a success that we entered into a more permanent venture with Charlestown Estates Limited, who prepared and provided the building for us – you know that the village is privately owned by that company? Roy and myself designed the downstairs layout, while Charlestown Estates designed the fabric and amenities of the building.

'After a lot of research it was decided to incorporate the multi-projection, audio-visual unit which, incidentally, was produced by a local Cornish firm, as an introduction to put visitors "into the picture" so to speak. That is a very expensive bit of equipment, incorporating some fourteen carousel slide projectors all of which may be called on simultaneously in the programme . . . and it really works!' he laughed.

'I personally started diving in 1947,' he continued, 'and did twenty-two years in the Royal Navy as a diver. One of my most interesting experiences – and you realise that after you've being doing the job that long you tend to overlook the romance and glamour side of the business – was when a navy team found the wreck of HMS *Association*, the flagship of Sir Clowdisley Shovell, which was wrecked on the Gilstone Ledges off the Scillies in 1707. I initiated that project, and it was a truly great moment when we finally identified remains of the ship which were scattered in depths from 30 feet down to 160 feet. The team had been searching across the years 1963 to 1967 – not an easy matter with the seas which run out there near Bishop's Rock lighthouse. In fact we've just written, with Peter McBride, another ex-Navy diver, a new book about it all entitled *Sir Clowdisley Shovell's Disaster*, which we published, and hopefully will be reprinted by the Conway Maritime Press.'

'What else are you working on at the moment?'

'One of my life's ambitions,' he replied, 'is to create and leave behind a record of every wreck which has ever occurred around the United Kingdom, from the very earliest records up to the present day. In the old days there was not any need to record wrecks, but this has become increasingly important as time passed. In fact we now have on our UK Shipwreck Computer Index details of over a quarter of a million wrecks since the 1100s. It involves an enormous amount of research as you may guess, but we're putting it all on computer.'

Just across St Austell Bay, within view of the busy white port of Par, is the tiny harbour of Polkerris. No commerce here, save that of pleasure boats which nose onto the beach in summer months to visit the Rashleigh Inn, or the 'Pub on the Beach' as it is known. The landlady, Mrs Kathryn Anne Harrower, was not at home, alas, when I lunched at this pleasant and flourishing pub, but her daughter Elizabeth took a few minutes from work to chat with me on one of the open terraces which abuts the beach . . . and a very congenial spot it is to sojourn with a glass of wine or beer, backed up by the excellent buffet provided at midday from within.

'Almost too congenial at the height of the season,' Elizabeth laughed. 'You can hardly get another boat nose-in to the sand down there, and there's often a queue at the doors! It is a popular spot for the staff of the China Clayworks to bring their customers, and we often have Chinese and Japanese folk as well as other nationalities here doing business over a meal.

SAPPHIRE FOWEY

Of course,' she added, 'the pub was not always in this building. It used to be in a cottage about fifty yards over there,' pointing towards the cliff to the north, 'until a storm washed it away.'

I understood then the reason for an exceptionally stout sea-wall which held up the terraces. 'This building,' she continued, glancing at the present pub, 'was a boatshed in those days, and the building on the other side of the slipway was the lifeboat house. Of course the lifeboat has gone, but they still use the slipway for launching pleasure craft, though mark you harbour dues must be paid to the agent of Menabilly Estate for the privilege. There is a painting somewhere done by Michael Kerris the artist whose studio is just up the road, of how the waterfront looked before that storm. It shows the pub as it was.'

Which was worth following up, so I tracked Michael Kerris down, busy with a blood-red paint-brush finishing off a most professional ACCOMMODATION notice obviously commissioned by a local guest house.

'You do commercial art as well?' I enquired, glancing round the studio where oil paintings hung by the score. He smiled. 'Not on a large scale, just now and then as a favour to locals. This is my real love . . . painting scenes on the coast and inland villages.'

'Elizabeth down at the pub tells me you've painted Polkerris waterfront as it looked before the original pub got swamped. Was it from your imagination or did you have a drawing or something to work from?'

'I did it from a very old photograph. It was quite a large painting I remember.'

'May I photograph it?'

'Sorry – sold and gone.'

But I tracked it down on the opposite coast, and from the two pictures you can see that, all-in-all, Polkerris hasn't changed much across a century or so.

Left: Mist over Polperro harbour.

Bill and Barbara Blamey of Polruan. 'It has its hazards keeping a guest house,' says Bill.

'Oh, it has its hazards,' responded Bill Blamey to my question, with more than a twinkle in his eye. I'd dropped in to number 18 Fore Street at Polruan because of the VACANCIES notice in the flower-bedecked window. Festooned as I was with cameras and a tape-recorder I must have looked like a geriatric Youth Employment Reject, but I wanted to get an insight into the life and philosophy of typical Cornish Guest House proprietors.

'Hazards . . . such as?' I queried, propping my bike against his clematis. Behind him I could see his wife Barbara with a skip-load of bedlinen.

'Well, just about everything happens if you're in this business long enough, and we've been in it for ten years. You sort of develop shock-absorbers that enable you to take things in your stride.'

'He was going upstairs to shave one day,' came Barbara's voice from the kitchen, 'when he was confronted by a stark naked female who said she was just coming down to ask if he'd heard the weather forecast. He never,' she muttered, 'told me what his answer was!'

'Shock-absorbers,' mused Bill, looking somewhere into the middle distance. 'Yes, we get 'em all. I remember one very nice little Japanese gentleman who booked in early but couldn't speak one word of English. He seemed to enjoy his breakfast, but we were a little worried when he went upstairs and, for half an hour, chanted prayers at the top of his voice. Well, I assume they were prayers, it didn't sound a bit like singing! A bit perplexing for the other guests, too, but it takes all sorts to make a world. Another strange thing about him,' he continued, 'when Barbara went up later in the day to change the bedlinen, she couldn't detect *which* of the two beds in the room he'd used. It was some days afterwards that it dawned on us: he used neither. He had slept on the floor with a sort of wooden dumb-bell as a pillow. He was carrying it when he arrived!'

The slipway, Toms Boatyard, Polruan.

'Certainly we get an enormous variety of types,' the two of them told me later as we took a cup of coffee onto the well-trimmed lawn behind Holly House. Below us was an incomparable view of Fowey harbour. 'Sometimes we are a little puzzled by the behaviour of the foreign guests . . . Strangely it's the Germans who stand out in our minds as the oddest. They often spend all day sleeping . . . never bother to go out and explore the village, or take the Ferry across to Fowey. If they book in for a week they sometimes stay around the house or garden all day. Even on the sunniest of days they stay in the bedroom all the time.'

'Sign of the age we live in,' Bill added, 'I would reckon that nine out of ten couples who book in nowadays are not married. We'd be very poor if we insisted on a marriage certificate!'

Bill is descended from a long line of Cornishmen, born and bred in Cornwall. He and Barbara have been married for quite a few years and, as he told me giving her a hug, 'she's now almost accepted as being one of we, 'spite of her foreign blood!'

A wood-turner by trade, Bill came back 'home' with Barbara to Cornwall after twenty-five years 'exile' in Surrey. 'With regards to our profession,' he explained, 'I think Cornwall lends itself to touring. Holidaymakers who come do, in general, want to keep on the move during the days they're here, so they do not wish to return to their chosen Guest House for an evening meal. This does particularly apply to Polruan where, thank goodness, we don't have beaches or entertainment facilities which attract mass hordes. But it's a fact that after twenty-four hours or so casual guests do tend to think they've "done" Polruan and they move on. But as you know it takes many weeks to thoroughly "do" any area of Cornwall. We have few local customers. I suppose

Fowey. View over 'Place' and the church.

most of our guests come from the Home Counties. The North and Wales are also well represented with, of course, quite a few from the Antipodes, America and Canada, plus some South Africans who come to Polruan because the Russell Inn was in the *Good Beer Guide*.'

'As a rule the guests are considerate and thoughtful, appreciative of the fact that they are sharing our home,' Barbara told me. 'Though, of course, one does get the odd exception. There was one lady who asked whether I'd mind if she brought her dog in with her because it was moulting and made the car in such a mess. It took me hours to rid the bedroom carpet of dog hairs!'

But it was quite clear to me that, despite the odd surprise, these two thoroughly enjoyed their calling. Bill still keeps his hand in at wood-turning with a splendid lathe which is housed in a shed at the top of his garden. I woke next morning to that most Cornish of sounds . . . the strident chatter of seagulls up on the roof ridge. The sun was already over the housetops and after a hearty breakfast I was ready for anything a Cornish spring day cared to provide!

Polruan is, quite simply in my opinion, a rarity. I

long ago fell in love with the steep, narrow streets which are not streets at all; with the numberless steps that lead sharply up and down from terrace to terrace, and above all with the surprise that constantly awaits when you turn and there, falling away below, is the magnificent river and the distant old town of Fowey spread out like a vast painting.

Evening is my favourite time. After perhaps a long walk on those imcomparable cliff paths past Lantic and Lantivet Bay to Polperro, you return tired but happy to this quaint and quite unspoilt Cornish village and chat with the locals as the sun sinks over Gribbin Head to the west. Then the river turns a deep, deep aquamarine, and the hulls and masts of yachts glow in the slanting light, and across the river comes the sound of church bells floating . . . and there is warmth and comfort and two friendly caring hosts back there where you will sleep tonight, for this is Cornwall – and Freedom – and what more, I ask, what more do you crave?

'I reckon,' came the slow American drawl, 'you've got about ten minutes before you'll need stilts.' Under the arches of Looe bridge I hastily focused for a final shot, stowed the camera and glanced at the river bed between me and the west-side quay. He was right, the creeping fingers of a rising tide were probing insidiously between the moorings, lifting fronds of green weed in rapidly expanding pools. The crabs were waking up.

Aboard a trim little sloop with the charming name *Composure*, and from beneath a wide-brimmed Stetson-type hat grinned a bearded face. 'We've just got time for a can of beer,' called Cecil Du Vale, musician from New Jersey. 'And what,' I asked him as I took off my shoes to wade ashore for another pint in the Harbour Moon, 'is an American in a Stetson, wearing a jacket emblazoned with "San Fransisco Police" doing in a Norman Pearn built yacht in Looe harbour? You look as if you've sort of taken root here.' At the top of the quayside steps Cecil stretched his arms and breathed deeply. A broad and happy grin split his face. 'The jacket? Oh, that's a buddy's cast-off . . . but me,' he laughed, 'I guess I'm just a very happy musician, a happy American musician who finds the quality of life here in Cornwall infinitely more attractive than back in the New Jersey area. Mind you I have to commute over there now and then to keep tabs on my studio . . . synthesizers and all that. Keyboard instruments chiefly . . . wrote a book myself: *Modern Harmony Using the Five-Note System*, and shortly I plan to bring the entire studio gear over here to Cornwall where I can work in a far more relaxed atmosphere.'

Curtis and Pape's boatyard, Looe. One may greet the souls of boats unborn here amid the wholesome scent of sawn wood.

'The quality of life in Cornwall is infinitely more attractive' he said. At Looe the fact proclaimed itself from every quay, every street . . . even from that comfortable pile of fish netting where a Cornish Maid is sunning herself in happy oblivion.

Low tide, west quay, Looe. 'I reckon you've got about ten minutes before you'll need stilts,' came the slow American drawl.

'Splendid name for your boat: *Composure*,' I commented, and he glowed, as all sailors – part-time or otherwise – will glow when you compliment their greatest love in life.

But there it was, from the musician's mouth so to speak: '. . . the quality of life in Cornwall is infinitely more attractive.' Do we not know what he is talking about? The fact proclaimed itself from every quay, every street, every heaped-up collection of lobster pots and . . . ah! from that comfortable pile of fish-netting where a Cornish Maid is sunning herself in happy oblivion!

This is Looe, and already the flowing tide is floating the dozens of small and not-so-small fishing boats. The shark-fishers are gathering up their gear and smelly chunks of ripe mackerel-bait, ready for another sortie out towards the Eddystone Light to rid the ocean of a few more 'bluenoses'.

But the port of Looe is more extensive than many visitors realise, for up-river of the fine bridge is a stretch of tidal estuary comparable to the Helford and the Fal. Explore there, where the swans glide on brackish water in regal and aloof elegance, and you will find on the west bank at the end of a somewhat rutted but quite enchanting lane, the boatyard of Frank Curtis and Pape Brothers Limited.

Boatyards have atmosphere, and the older, more long-established yards have their own unique character which distinguishes them from any other yard. It's something to do with the air of woodcraft which lingers about them; the smell of sawn timber and shavings which carpet the floor, and the tier upon tier of apparently haphazard but, in fact, very carefully sorted pieces which, some future day, will be *exactly* the part one needs to replace that rotten frame or breast-hook in old Charlie's clinker punt. And seasoned to a marvellous hardness too, unlike this instant-grown modern muck that shrinks and warps before you can so much as throw it away!

Everywhere you look on the ground floor of Curtis and Pape's yard is a motley collection of 'useful pieces'. To the uninitiated eye it might appear a sort of wholesome chaos: to those who work here each area is laid aside for storing a piece of wood with some quality which distinguishes it from what may look like an identical piece elsewhere. It's a wonderful place to browse, given permission, for it strikes the eye of an artist as a rich tapestry in sepia. One almost greets the souls of boats unborn there amid the clutter. Long may such 'clutter' be with us, increasingly 'standardised' species that we tend to become!

But upstairs it is a rather different scene. Here the new medium of glassfibre is in full sway, and indeed it was in this very yard that Chay Blyth's famous trimaran *Brittany Ferries* was built. He won the Singlehanded Transatlantic Race in her. 'Nice chap, too,' said Mick Marshall, Managing Director of the firm. 'Straight as a die to deal with; knew exactly what he wanted and he got it . . . she was a very good boat.'

'Tell me about the firm,' I prompted.

'It was started by my father-in-law, Frank Curtis. A wonderful chap. I'm talking now of some fifty years or more back, and of course in those days they built solely of wood. The business prospered, and during the last war this yard was employing about three thousand men, chiefly on contracts for the Admiralty. But like all boatyards the recession has forced us to cut down considerably on our work force. Most of our orders today are for specific customers, one-off craft with personal interior design layouts.'

'Do you build in steel?'

Mick looked across to where, under the trees outside the yard, a brand new gleaming white forty-five foot ocean-goer was propped on temporary 'legs'. 'She's one of our designs,' he told me, 'though that boat wasn't actually built in this yard.'

Up on her foredeck I could just see a blue woollen bobble cap above some curls, and was about to hail the lady when a car rolled to a halt beside me. Out of it stepped a sprightly gentleman who was quite evidently the skipper. 'We're fitting her out ourselves,' he told me, 'and then sailing her across to the USA via the Trade Route. We propose to sell her there, not because that was the original plan,' he added a little ruefully, 'but since the adventure was conceived the cost of everything has rocketted so much we've no option. We have to sell, to pay off the loans, and today if you're fortunate, one can, in the USA, get just about twice the price for a British built boat that you would manage to raise here in the UK.'

'And then?'

'Then . . . well, maybe we'll just come back and do the same thing all over again, but this time with the ready money!'

So it goes, and one wonders where it will all end, the seemingly ever-increasing cost of things. But this is a far cry from the glory of a spring day in Looe, and a problem which will have to be faced by such as this sandy-bottomed trojan imp who's doing a 'Canute' with the waves back there on the beach . . . and it's all a part of the rich pattern of living.

Hiding under the steep wooded headland are the hamlets of Kingsand and Cawsand.

The coast road from Looe through Seaton, Downderry, Portwrinkle and Crafthole is a delight. Mark you, anything larger than a Sinclair C5 plus a powerful pair of legs might be a hazard in places, especially if you tackle the hill at the west end of Portwrinkle, but it's fun. The worst that can happen if you are travelling eastward is that you land up in the waters of Whitsand Bay, and you could be baptised in worse places for it was here that Drake and Howard faced the Spanish Armada and took the wind from their sails.

About half a mile offshore is the wreck of an American ship, the *James Egan Lane* – only an American could have a name as fine as that – which was torpedoed in March 1945. Her mast used to be visible from the crosstrees upwards, and I've spent many an entranced minute holding onto it while peering from *Lugworm*, trying unsuccessfully to make out the line of her hull down there in the green depths. The mast has gone now, I note, but she is a favourite spot for fishermen. Why? Fish love wrecks, especially conger-eels. After the war I spent five years blowing up sunken wrecks that littered the shipping lanes, and each time we blasted up came a few congers, caught playing hide-and-seek in and out of the portholes. Cod, too, thousands of them, but it's a rotten and unfair way to fish and I wish we could have done it all in some different fashion. Most of the *James Egan Lane*'s cargo has been salvaged, but she is still a popular venue for sub-aqua divers.

If you look ashore, up on the high ground backing the coast is the low, grey bastion of Tregantle Fort, looking like a film-set for *Beau Geste* and the French Foreign Legion. No hardboard and prefabricated bay windows in those days: just ton after ton of solid stone, and what a job it must have been carting it all up there. The small square building you see atop Rame Head is a fourteenth-century chapel dedicated to St Michael, the patron saint of Cornwall. How fitting it is that he should be represented here, for this is the first and the last headland on the Cornish coastline, and he's casting a watchful eye across there toward Devon, for you never quite know what they'm up to!

We are near the end of our journey now, for just around the corner, hiding under the steep, wooded flanks of the headland, are the waterside hamlets of Cawsand and Kingsand. They are not all that easy to reach by road unless you happen to be travelling

The mighty Tamar which almost links hands with Marsland Water which is where we started this journey. What better place to view it than from the stately wooded greensward of Mount Edgcumbe?

'Oh, me 'andsome, we'm some lucky . . . eh?'

from Looe, as we have come, but they are well worth visiting. They have an almost Italian atmosphere, much akin to the small Mediterranean ports of Porto and Sperlonga, though a deal colder when I took photographs by early morning sunlight. There is left now only Picklecombe Fort, which has been converted into flats, down there on the foreshore, for we are inside Plymouth Sound and greeting the mighty Tamar. This adventure started far up this river very near to its source where it all but links hands with Marsland Water. Full circle, almost, we have come, and what better place to end a journey than the stately greensward of Mount Edgcumbe?

A friend of mine, Cornish to his toenails, when speaking once of this lovely estate said: '. . . but I always feel it's not really Cornwall.' I know exactly what he means. Up here beneath the tall and elegant trees, looking across the sloping fields of well-grazed grass to the dockyards opposite, it is indeed a far cry from those windswept dry-stone 'hedges' spattered with sea-pinks and wild campion, from the spiky gorse and granite outcrops washed by the restless ocean and backed by lonely moors.

But Mount Edgcumbe is Cornwall all the same. It is as much Cornwall as are those man-made white mountains of the china clay works, and the slate quarries, and the underground tunnels of the tin mines. All these help to make up that rich pattern which unquestionably forms the premier region of Britain.

As for we who live here . . .

'Oh, me 'andsome, we'm some lucky . . . eh?'

ALSO AVAILABLE

SEA STORIES OF CORNWALL
by Ken Duxbury

THE CORNISH COUNTRYSIDE
by Sarah Foot

RIVERS OF CORNWALL
by Sarah Foot

WEST CORNWALL IN THE OLD DAYS
by Douglas Williams

PEOPLE AND PLACES IN CORNWALL
by Michael Williams

100 YEARS AROUND THE LIZARD
by Jean Stubbs

125 YEARS WITH THE WESTERN MORNING NEWS
by James Mildren

HEALING HARMONY AND HEALTH
by Barney Camfield

AROUND BUDE AND STRATTON
by Joan Rendell

MOUNT'S BAY
by Douglas Williams

100 YEARS ON BODMIN MOOR
by E. V. Thompson

WESTCOUNTRY MYSTERIES
Introduced by Colin Wilson

AROUND LAND'S END
by Michael Willams

NORTH CORNWALL IN THE OLD DAYS
by Joan Rendell

DISCOVERING CORNWALL'S SOUTH COAST
by E. V. Thompson

SEA STORIES OF DEVON
Introduced by E. V. Thompson

AROUND GLORIOUS DEVON
by David Young

DARTMOOR IN THE OLD DAYS
by James Mildren

SOMERSET IN THE OLD DAYS
by David Young

LEGENDS OF SOMERSET
by Sally Jones

CURIOSITIES OF SOMERSET
by Lornie Leete-Hodge

UNKNOWN SOMERSET
by Rosemary Clinch and Michael Willams

UNKNOWN DEVON
by Rosemary Anne Lauder, Michael Willams and Monica Wyatt

THE CRUEL CORNISH SEA
by David Mudd

CORNISH CHURCHES
by Joan Rendell

STRANGE SOMERSET STORIES
Introduced by David Foot

KING ARTHUR COUNTRY IN CORNWALL
by Brenda Duxbury, Michael Williams and Colin Wilson

LEGENDS OF CORNWALL
by Sally Jones

MYSTERIES IN THE DEVON LANDSCAPE
by Michael Williams

PEOPLE AND PLACES IN DEVON
by Monica Wyatt

We shall be pleased to send you our catalogue giving full details of our growing list of titles in Devon, Cornwall and Somerset and forthcoming publications.

If you have difficulty in obtaining our titles, write to Bossiney Books, Land's End, St Teath, Bodmin, Cornwall.